basic Rhythm
Programming

T0084367

Printed and bound in Great Britain by Antony Rowe Limited, Chippenham, Wiltshire

Published in the UK by SMT, an imprint of Sanctuary Publishing Limited, Sanctuary House, 45-53 Sinclair Road, London W14 0NS, United Kingdom

www.sanctuarypublishing.com

Copyright: © Mark Roberts 2003

All rights reserved. No part of this book may be reproduced in any form or by any electronic or mechanical means, including information storage or retrieval systems, without permission in writing from the publisher, except by a reviewer, who may quote brief passages.

While the publishers have made every reasonable effort to trace the copyright owners for any or all of the photographs in this book, there may be some omissions of credits, for which we apologise.

ISBN: 1-84492-008-9

basic Rhythm Programming

Mark Roberts

smt

ACKNOWLEDGEMENTS

Thank you to the following for all their help and support:

Nataša, Mum and Dad, Jean and Anthony, Dr Bob Lockie, Alex Mungo, Mio and Bosa, Mags, Peter Cunnah, Kevin, Adrian Hardy, Euan Hill, Bias, Tom Medows, The Sitar Tandoori, Alistair Fincham and all the guys at Panic.

Simon Jayes at Pearl; Tina Clarke at Zildjian; Risto at Arbiters; Peter Button at Clinton's Solicitors; Louise King, Pat Reed and Kevin Lowery at *Rhythm* magazine; Ronan Macdonald at *Computer Music* magazine; James Cumpsty; and Sanctuary Publishing – Chris Bradford, Iain MacGregor and Penny Braybrooke, and special thanks to Alan Heal.

ABOUT THE AUTHOR

Mark's experience as a professional drummer is extensive and varied. He has been a professional drummer for 17 years and a drum programmer for the last ten. He has played for (amongst others) Massive Attack, D:Ream, Neneh Cherry, The Godfathers and DJ Rap (drummer and musical director). Mark has been a regular contributor to *Rhythm* magazine since 1995 and has focused on introducing drummers to cutting-edge styles and technology. He has held the position of Head of Contemporary Styles on a groundbreaking Popular Music Performance university degree course and has been involved in the development and subsequent accreditation of popular music courses at BMus level. Mark co-owns Panic Music, one of the most innovative rehearsal, recording and educational facilities in London.

Mark is endorsed by Pearl, Zildjian, Vic Firth and Protection Racket.

CONTENTS

INTRODUCTION

The aim of this book is to introduce anyone who wants to program drums in a modern computer-music environment, whether they are a musician or not, to the way a drummer thinks and to demystify the art of drumming. Throughout, you'll find tips and techniques to help you not only to understand how modern rhythms are put together but how they can be manipulated.

Rhythm Programming does not affiliate itself to any one sequencing package. Instead, the aim is to give the reader the knowledge of common rhythm-manipulation techniques and concepts found in all music-sequencing applications. Once a basic understanding of how rhythms are put together and manipulated is achieved, the software becomes merely a tool to aid rhythmic creativity.

The book is split into seven chapters, all of which are designed to function independently of each other. Relevant chapters can be viewed according to a particular task that the user needs to perform.

Chapter 1: MIDI Recording

This chapter deals with the recording and editing of MIDI information. Although this book is by definition biased towards drum sounds, many of the programming techniques and theories explored here apply to all MIDI instruments.

Chapter 2: Musicality And Music Theory

For anyone who has no formal understanding of rhythm, I have explained the basic concepts of groove creation and rhythmic subdivision as applied to programming.

Chapter 3: Audio Recording 1

This chapter covers the concept of creating your own source sounds. Relying on pre-recorded samples and loops is a constant feature of drum programming, but it's also extremely important to create and manipulate your own sounds. This chapter will introduce you to the audio-recording process, highlighting the technical aspects of getting drum audio into your computer and the nature of what to look for in drum audio. Feel, groove, tuning, kit setups and microphone placement are all discussed.

Chapter 4: Audio Recording 2

This chapter covers the manipulation of recorded and imported audio and covers creating and editing loops, what to look for in a loop and how to synchronise loops with your MIDI information using audio-correction functions. Also, the practice of creating and editing rhythms from single audio drum hits is fully explained.

Chapter 5: Working With MIDI And Audio

This chapter looks closely at the audio output and input paths. The interaction between audio and MIDI information is explained, again with the use of interactive tutorials and screengrabs.

Chapter 6: Styles

This chapter details the programming idiosyncrasies of the most popular current trends in music, including hip-hop, modern R&B, drum and bass, rock, funk, Latin, techno, trance, garage and dance. The drum sounds associated with each genre are explained in detail and specific programming tutorials have been added where necessary.

Chapter 7: Programming in Odd Times

This chapter covers drum programming in rhythms other than standard 4/4. Throughout, tutorials explain the programming traits associated with odd time signatures and audio and MIDI examples are provided to demonstrate the feel and attitude of each rhythm.

1 MIDI RECORDING

The concept of recording MIDI is a fairly straightforward process. With any fairly modern MIDI-compatible synth and a desktop computer or dedicated hardware sequencer, you should have access to a large palette of sounds to program. Of course, you'll need to set things up first so that you're sending and receiving MIDI information through your sequencer. This will give you the ability to record MIDI data onto the main Arrange page of your sequencer and trigger the sound module of your choice.

First, though, a word of warning: different sequencing packages look different, employing particular graphical representation, and although you'll need to access exactly the same parameters during operation, the way in which you access them will vary from sequencer to sequencer. The main thing is to understand what individual parameters you're looking for, what they do and why you need to use them in the programming process.

At the time of writing, Steinberg's Cubase VST and SX and Emagic's Logic Audio are industry-standard software sequencing packages, and both utilise the same approach in the recording and representation of recorded MIDI and audio, whether you're recording drums or any other instrument. You'll find that I've used selective screenshots from these packages to illustrate particular sections of the book, but I must stress that it's the programming theory and why certain methods of recording and editing are employed that's most important.

The Arrange Page

After booting up your sequencer by double-clicking on its icon on your computer's hard drive, you'll be taken directly into your sequencer's main Arrange page, which is an autoload default page. Any custom settings you make, such as MIDI and audio assignments, can be saved as this file name and they will always be pre-assigned whenever you start any new recording.

When you record a song or arrangement, it's wise to go to the File menu and save it, naming it appropriately. Make sure that you direct your file to be saved in a place where you'll be able to find it again. Over the page are screenshots of Arrange pages in Cubase and Logic Audio, two of the most popular sequencer packages. No matter what form of recording you're doing, you'll need to be aware of the parameters listed here.

basic Rhythm Programming

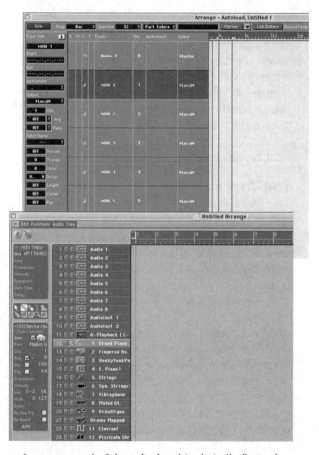

Arrange pages in Cubase (top) and Logic Audio (bottom)

The Arrange page is where most of your main recording and monitoring will take place. One of the most significant breakthroughs that came with the switch from traditional tape recording to the virtual world of computer recording is that now, instead of being totally reliant on tape counters, your whole arrangement is displayed in front of you, graphically, on your computer.

Before I guide you through the MIDI recording process, it's worth defining the various elements of a typical Arrange page setup. The Arrange page in Cubase has a bar indicator strip at the top and a red arrow with a line running down to the bottom of the page. This is the position indicator, and its job is to track the bar position as you play through your arrangement.

To the left of the main Cubase Arrange page is a Track List. This will show you a default number of audio and MIDI tracks.

To the left of the track list are four additional columns marked A, M, C and T, and these relate to their own individual track on the Arrange page and provide the following functions:

- **A** is your Activity column, indicating recorded MIDI and audio activity on a track-by-track basis.

- **M** is the Mute and Solo column, which gives you the ability to silence any of your recorded MIDI or audio material, either track by track or globally by clicking on the Solo button situated on the top-right-hand corner of your Arrange page or by pressing the letter S on your keyboard.

- **C** stands for *track class*, which is an extremely important function and essential to the recording process. The track class you choose will determine the type of track you record or monitor. There are many different track classes available, although for the purposes of this book we will only be concerning ourselves with audio tracks, MIDI tracks, drum tracks and mixer tracks.

- **T** is the time-locked column. This means that the events recorded onto that particular track will not move even if the tempo is changed.

The Transport Bar

This bar basically reads the same for both Cubase and Logic. In the centre block of the bar, you'll see the main transport functions, represented by Fast-Forward, Rewind, Play, Stop and Record buttons. The Transport bar icon will also incorporate Punch In, Punch Out, Cycle Record and Playback options, as well as Overdub and

Replace Record modes. You are able to alter the positions of the right and left locators, and you can view your song position either numerically in bar format or in seconds, the latter of which is normally used for film and TV work.

Transport bars in Cubase (top) and Logic Audio (bottom)

Punching In And Out

The left and right locator flags can be set to any position within the main Arrange page, either by punching in your desired positions, by double-clicking on the L(eft) and R(ight) boxes on the Transport bar and entering your locator positions on the computer keyboard, or by clicking and dragging the L and R flags across the Arrange page.

The Punch In and Punch Out icons are situated at the bottom-left-hand side of the Transport bar. If the Punch

In icon is illuminated during the recording process, as soon as the positional indicator makes contact with the left locator, the sequencer will automatically start recording. If the Punch Out indicator is illuminated, the sequencer will automatically drop out of Record as soon as the song position makes contact with the right locator. Both Punch In and Punch Out are extremely useful functions, particularly if you want to start and stop the recording process over a specific number of bars in the middle of your drum arrangement.

Cycle Mode

Also located in the Transport bar is the button that activates Cycle mode. This function can be used during your sequencer's Play mode or during the recording process.

Cycle Play

Once you've clicked on the Cycle icon and it's illuminated, you're in Cycle mode, which allows you to loop the portion of your arrangement situated between your left and right locators.

Cycle Record

Once you've dropped into Record, as soon as the bar indicator hits the right locator, it will immediately return to the left locator and start its cycle again.

Record Mode

There are two types of record mode which are normally used during the recording process: Overdub and Replace.

Overdub

When the sequencer is in Overdub mode, every time you record information onto one track, the new recording is added to the previous one. Overdub mode is extremely useful when combined with Cycle mode, as the sequencer will cycle between your locator positions and you can effectively create your rhythm by adding a new voice with every new cycle.

Replace

When the sequencer is in Replace mode, each time you start recording you will be replacing all of your previously recorded information.

Quantise

Over the course of the book, the theory of quantise will become more apparent. In its basic form, quantise is a correction facility that adjusts recorded material to its nearest musical subdivision. The required subdivision is chosen from a drop-down box situated at the top of the main Arrange page. Both Cubase and Logic allow you to quantise both recorded MIDI and audio information. The quantise function is one of the main

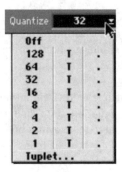

Selecting a quantise value in Cubase

tools you'll be using when you program any rhythm, and its creative use will allow you to play with the groove and timing of your rhythms, giving you ultimate flexibility.

Logic Audio and Cubase both have drop-down Quantise menus which allow you to access various default quantise settings. By using Match and Groove Quantise, you can create your own individual quantise settings that can be applied to your programmed rhythmic information.

Snap
Snap is an editing facility which is extensively used by all sequencing packages, and its use becomes apparent

if you have to cut or move any recorded information around the Arrange page and when you have to edit individual notes in any of the editors. Once you've selected the relevant timing division for the Snap function, when you move a piece of information, it will automatically snap to the nearest subdivision to its left or right. Snap also applies if you wanted to cut any recorded blocks of information using the scissors in your toolbox.

Here's an example of Snap in action. If you activated the Snap To Bar function, you wouldn't be able to move any piece of recorded MIDI or audio information (which appears as blocks, once recorded) around the main Arrange page or any of the associated editors in any other division than a bar. The Snap function can be set to all the divisions shown overleaf, and it can also be turned off completely – this means that information can be moved anywhere within the Arrange page. Turning Snap off isn't always advisable, however, because, if you wanted to join two pieces of information together, it would be impossible to join them exactly and would take an inordinate amount of time to ensure that there were no timing errors when the two pieces were played back. However, turning off the Snap function works well with some types of audio material, such as strings or vocals floating over the main drum track.

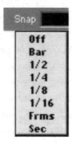

The Cubase Snap menu

In the main MIDI Editor, Snap works slightly differently in that it also allows you to move notes around, enabling you to edit grooves of different Snap subdivisions, changing the grid of the edit page on which you're working.

The Inspector

The Inspectors in both Cubase and Logic are accessed by clicking on the arrow icon situated at the bottom-left-hand corner of the main Arrange page and provide information about a highlighted track, allowing you to alter parameters relating to the information programmed on that track.

Moving from the top of the Inspector down are the following criteria:

- **Track Name**

- **Instrument** – This will tell you the name of the instrument set to play on your selected track. The instrument name can be typed in when you select the Setup Instruments dialog box.

- **Output** – This dialog box shows you which external sound module or internal synth is receiving MIDI trigger information.

- **Channel** – This tells you the MIDI channel that you have selected for a particular track.

- **Bank Change** and **Program Change** – These functions allow you to scroll through different banks of individual sounds on your chosen MIDI synth or external module from the Arrange page. They also allow you to include program changes in your arrangement – for example, you could have one drum sound for the verse of your arrangement and, by pressing Record and selecting another program, you could select another kit sound for your chorus. Rogue Program Change messages can become extremely annoying, though, so make sure you're not scrolling through programs aimlessly while you're recording.

basic Rhythm Programming

Inspectors in Logic (left) and Cubase (right)

- **Patch Name** – This allows you to scroll through synth patches by name rather than by number. Although functions 4, 5 and 6 are extremely useful and patch names are automatically set when you use VST instruments, I prefer to scroll through sounds using the data wheel of the external module I'm working with or the cursor keys on the synth itself. There's nothing more annoying than coming up against an endless list of names that mean relatively little until you hear them. It's much easier to scroll back and forth through sounds by hand rather than use the mouse and have to negotiate a long-winded drop-down menu.

The following criteria relate to Logic Audio.

- **Volume** – This function allows you to change the levels of each track or part.

- **Transpose** – By using the Transpose function, you can change the pitch of the instruments assigned to a particular track.

- **Velocity** – This function changes the dynamics of the MIDI data being triggered from a particular track.

- **Delay** – Delay can be used in rhythm programming to alter the feel of a particular drum part – for example, a snare part can be shifted to a position slightly earlier or later in a sequence, or a drum part can be made to sit with a bass part. The delay function applies to the highlighted track and its value is noted in 16th notes and ticks. (One 16th note is 3840 ticks.)

- **Length** – This is noted as a percentage and can be used to shorten or lengthen triggered sounds. An example of this would be using the Length function to shorten a long bass-drum sound or thinning out a snare drum to give more space to a MIDI drum groove.

- **Compression** – This facility can be used in conjunction with the Velocity function to even out parts of an arrangement – for example, if a shaker part sounded uneven, you could use the compression function to make it sound a little smoother.

- **Pan** – This function enables you to place a particular part in the stereo image. R63 is extreme right, L63 is extreme left.

- **Multi Out** – This function allows you to assign multiple MIDI channels to be triggered from the MIDI information contained within a track. This means that you can layer sounds and MIDI information contained within one track with other external or internal sound sources that have been assigned to other MIDI channels. An example of this would be locking a bass drum assigned to MIDI channel 10 to a bass guitar assigned to MIDI channel 6; the two voices will trigger information contained on the same track at exactly the same time.

Groove And Feel

MIDI recording is a very different process from the recording of audio, as you always have to bear in mind that you're triggering information from a sound source, whether this is an internal soft synth, an external module or sounds housed within a keyboard. Therefore, in order to make sense of your recorded rhythms, you'll have to tie all of your MIDI recordings to a tempo and time signature in order for them to work. However, there are a number of key points to remember before you can even start the recording process, which will enable your rhythms to have groove, feel and direction.

First of all, how long is your recording going to be? When you use any sequencing package, it's best to limit your recording to small two- or four-bar chunks, as it's impossible to arrange a long rambling MIDI drum or percussion part effectively. The editing and structuring facilities on all modern software-based sequencers will allow you to edit and copy individual two- or four-bar grooves as many times as required in order to complete an arrangement. The main thing to remember, concerning the length of your initial groove, is that it's far better to have a two-bar pattern that totally works and fits the song than to have a longer pattern with dud notes and inconsistent dynamics that will take you hours to edit and tidy up.

Groove

Basically, a groove can be defined as a repetitive drum part that, once set up, constitutes the backbone of a track. Within popular music, the drums are traditionally the driving force of an arrangement and create the framework that the more melodic instruments can either lock with or weave in and out of.

Feel

Defining the term *feel* probably constitutes a book in itself. A musician's feel is his or her own individual voice, and modern sequencers allow you a tremendous amount of flexibility where feel is concerned. Each genre of music will have its own particular type of groove associated with it, and how that particular groove is executed would be defined as *feel*. Many traditional musicians are heard saying that machines have no feel and that all programmed rhythms sound stale and stagnant. This is not true, of course, and really sounds like they're missing the point. If it *was* true, you could say that no one could play music unless they'd been formally trained, which is clearly not the case. Music knows no rules, and since the advent of computers and sequencers whole new genres of music have evolved with computer-driven feels and grooves forming an integral part of their sound. In fact, if live drums were played with this music, they would sound completely wrong for the track.

Reference

The best way to achieve a competent MIDI recording is to have an idea of what you're trying to achieve, so it would be a good idea to reference some previously recorded material in the musical genre in which you're working. This will enable you to identify a number of crucial elements that will make your recording sound like the way you hear it in your head.

Choosing Sounds

Every musical genre will have particular sounds associated with it and an individual programming style. Certain fields of music will be constructed exclusively by MIDI information triggering single drum and percussion hits housed within internal and external modules, others will be totally live, audio-based styles and some will use combinations of single sounds programmed in the MIDI domain to formulate the basic pattern and then use live audio to provide ambience, some feel and dynamics.

Tempo

The *tempo* of a track is basically how fast or slow it is, determined by the tempo value on the Transport bar. The tempo is the speed of a piece of music, and in the context of sequencers it's usually measured in bpm (beats per minute).

Time Signatures

As with tempo, it's worth defining the term *time signature*. The time signature of a piece determines the number of beats in each bar and the way in which those notes are grouped – for instance, in a bar of 4/4, the first 4 informs you that there are four beats in each bar, while the second 4 indicates that the beat values are quarter notes (crotchets). A large percentage of music genres will have a particular time signature and tempo associated with them, so before you start recording, it's worth having a listen to your reference material and tapping along with the piece and then matching that with the click on your sequencer's Transport bar. Of course, working out the time signature of a piece is slightly more complicated than this, although most popular music grooves are written in 4/4, which is the default time signature for all sequencers. The subject of time signatures will be covered in greater detail in Chapter 2, 'Musicality And Music Theory', and in Chapter 7, 'Programming In Odd Times'.

Recording MIDI

Your recording will take place on your sequencer's main Arrange page, where recorded material is represented as blocks. These blocks span the number of bars for which your recording lasted.

Connecting Your System

First, make sure that you're sending and receiving MIDI information and that your MIDI Thru function is activated. You can check this by going into the Options menu (in Cubase) and selecting MIDI Setup and ensuring that the 'MIDI Thru' box is ticked. You can see if you're receiving and transmitting by checking out the MIDI Activity indicator on the Transport bar in both Cubase and Logic.

Setting Your Click

As I've stated before, when recording MIDI-triggered rhythms it's extremely important that you use the sequencer's click track as a guide. If your recording is out of time with the sequencer, you won't be able to make use of any of the editing facilities, and as your arrangement grows and you start to add more parts,

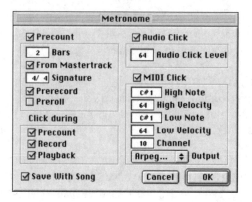

Click Set-Up dialog box in Cubase

it will sound worse. Also, if you want to extend your arrangement, you'll find it impossible to copy parts accurately, and if you need to transfer your arrangement to another studio, it will be almost impossible to lock it to another arrangement.

The click dialog offers you the following options:

- **Precount** – This allows you to select the number of bars of click you want to hear before the sequencer starts to record. Ticking the 'Precount' box activates this function.

- **Time Signature** – If you're working in a time signature other than 4/4, you'll need your click to reflect this if you want your recording to make sense. To change the time signature, click on the 'Time Signature' box using the mouse and nudge its value up or down. Alternatively, you can double-click on the 'Time Signature' box and enter in a new value using the numeric keypad.

The Click Track dialog box also offers you options relating to when you want to hear your click (ie during the Precount) while recording and during playback, and ticking the appropriate boxes will activate these functions. You can also choose the output you want to hear your click from, which by default is set to C1, MIDI channel 10. The default for drums, meanwhile, is MIDI channel 10 and C1 is a normally a default rimshot sound.

Track Class

To select a Track Class, first select a track to record onto by clicking on it with the mouse. Click on it again to name it. Once you've named the track, pressing the Return key on the computer keyboard will translate to all parts created on that track.

Next, select the class of track you require by pulling down the Track Class menu in the Arrange page and

basic Rhythm Programming

Selecting a track class

selecting the type of track you require. (In Cubase, the Track Class column is located in the main Arrange page and is marked 'C'.) There are two types of MIDI tracks to choose from in the Track Class column: MIDI tracks (indicated by a note symbol) and drum tracks (which carry a drumstick icon). The difference between these two tracks lies mainly in the formats of their edit pages.

The logical conclusion may be to create a drum track specifically for the recording, which is a good idea but actually makes little difference to the recording process, as it occurs on the main Arrange page. Initially, most programmers – unless they're drummers by trade – stick to the main MIDI track note icon, which is the method I'll be using here. MIDI tracks are extremely flexible they can be changed into drum tracks simply by changing the Track Class icon. (This procedure does not apply to the conversion of audio tracks into MIDI tracks.)

Next, set your locator positions to a length of two or four bars, as described earlier, and activate your click.

Overdub Or Replace

As I mentioned earlier, when your sequencer is set to Overdub, as you continue to record on the same track, your new MIDI hits will be added to your previously recorded MIDI information. Replace mode indicates that all new MIDI data will overwrite all of the previously recorded information on that track.

Starting A Recording

When you press the Record button on the Transport bar, the sequencer will give you a click intro (set to two bars in the default setup) and the recording will take place from the left locator position. As soon as the recording has started, you can play your information into your sequencer. Depending on what record mode you've chosen, the sequencer will either stop recording as soon as it hits the left locator (Punch Out) or it will continue to cycle between the right and left locator positions (Cycle Record).

Once the recording is complete, press the Stop icon. Rewind your song-position indicator back to the left locator (using the Rewind button on the Transport bar) and click on the Play icon (also on the Transport bar). This operation can also be achieved by clicking on the Stop button a second time, which will also return your song position bar to the left locator's position. Your MIDI information will be represented by a block of information on the Arrange page.

At this stage, it's important to name your tracks and parts, as the more complex your arrangement becomes, the harder it will be to pinpoint which sounds are being triggered by which particular block of information. Also, if you come back to an arrangement after some time, you'll have a laborious task ahead of you if none of your sounds or tracks are named. Your recorded information will play back independently of any other recorded MIDI information as long as it has been assigned to a different MIDI channel. Audio information obeys a completely different set of rules, however, and will not be influenced in any way by other tracks.

Finally, if you aren't satisfied with your new recording, you can delete it by pressing the Backspace key on the computer keyboard.

Editing On The Arrange Page

All modern sequencer packages rely on a combination of parameters to allow the user to enhance and manipulate recorded MIDI information. This is done by using a series of editors, the Quantise and Snap functions and the sequencer's own selection of tools, which vary depending on whether you're manipulating information on the main Arrange page or you're working in one of the editors.

The Cubase Toolbox
Pointer

The default tool is the Pointer. This allows you to move your information blocks within the Arrange page, with the precise placement of blocks that you move determined by the Snap setting, which will automatically place your move to the nearest subdivision, depending on the setting you've chosen. For example, if the Snap value is set to a bar, you'll be able to move your information only to the start of a bar, nowhere else. The Snap values run from Snap To A Bar to Off, although these values can be changed at any time during the editing process according to your requirements.

Scissors

The Scissors tool allows you to cut up your blocks of recorded information. For example, if you recorded a long drum groove over eight bars and decided that most of it was unwanted except for the middle two bars, you could use the scissors tool to chop away unwanted material, leaving you with your shortened drum part.

At this point, I will stress again that adhering to your click during the recording process is essential for quick and efficient editing. If your recorded information is out of sync with the sequencer's click, you'll have an awful job locating and subsequently cutting away unwanted information. For example, if you've recorded eight bars of information and you want to keep bars 3–5, set your Snap value to Snap To Bar and simply

The Cubase toolbox

cut at the beginning of bar 3 and the beginning of bar 6 (if the chosen Snap To Bar value won't let you cut anywhere but the beginning of a bar), and your edit will be done in seconds. However, if the recorded MIDI rhythm doesn't match the sequencer's click track, it could take you ages to line up the start of your groove to an appropriate Snap value and may require you to open up an editor to put the groove right. Basically, in most cases, prevention is better than cure!

Pencil

With the pencil tool, you can either draw in blank information blocks that are tied to existing blocks of information or copy a block of information and paste it into another location. The copy will be attached to the original, and once again the Snap function will allow the copy to end exactly at the beginning of a bar. To move a block of recorded information, place the Pencil at the end of the block, click the mouse button and drag the end of the block to its new position.

Eraser

The Eraser tool, as its name suggests, allows you to erase any unwanted blocks of information either by clicking on them or by holding down the mouse button, 'drawing' around a selection of information blocks and then clicking on them.

Mute

The Mute function is denoted by an 'X' and this allows you to silence a particular part situated on a track. This is an extremely useful tool when arranging information – you might want to try muting a particular part of your drum arrangement to allow other elements of your rhythm to breathe. There is also a Global Mute button, but this will mute your whole track, as opposed to an individual block of information situated within a track.

Speaker

Selecting the speaker icon and dragging it over a part will allow you to pick out and reference the individual notes contained within a block of information.

Quantise

The Quantise tool will allow you to 'match quantise' the note placement of one part with that of another. This function applies to both audio and MIDI tracks, and it can be extremely useful. An example of this would be matching a complex bass-drum pattern with a bass part. To use this function, select the 'Q' function from the tool box and drag the relevant bass part over the bass-drum part you wish to be matched. The Quantise parameter box situated at the top of the Arrange page will determine the number of notes that will be affected.

Choosing a quantise value of 8 or 16 will allow the main bass-drum hits to be matched to your bass part while all non-essential notes will remain intact. When you use the Match Quantise function, a dialog box will appear asking you if you'd like to include accents, which would tie the velocity of the two parts together. Sometimes this is unnecessary, particularly if you want the groove of your two parts to be tied but you don't want this to extend to every inflection.

Glue

The Glue tool is used to join two parts together. To do this, select the Glue icon from the toolbox, place it over the part situated to the left of the part that you wish to stick to it and click the two parts will be automatically joined together. This process is particularly useful when you need to join a number of parts together, allowing you to move around an arrangement as one big block rather than laboriously move tiny blocks of information from one place to another. The joining process applies to all of the parts situated on a track.

Magnifying Glass

All sequencing packages will allow you to expand and contract parts and windows. The magnifying tool enables you to increase or decrease in size a particular part, making for easier editing.

MIDI Editors

The two main editors used in the creation of MIDI drum grooves are the Key Editor and the Drum Editor. (Logic users will be familiar with the Matrix Editor, which actually looks almost identical to Cubase's Key Edit page.) In Cubase, the editor you access is determined by the relevant Track Class icon Key Edit is represented by a musical note and Drum Edit is indicated by a drumstick icon. Both of these Track Class settings should be chosen before you start the recording process, although you can switch between editor screen sets after your recording is completed. The Track Class dialog box is located in the Track Class column, located on the left of the main Arrange page.

Key Edit/Matrix Editor

You can open the Key Edit window in one of three ways: you can double-click on the block of recorded information you wish to change, you can go to the main Toolbar and choose 'Edit' from the Edit menu or you can use a keyboard shortcut.

Key Edit is normally used by keyboard players who need to see not only the location but also the pitch and duration of their recorded material. Once you're inside the Key Edit page, you'll see your recorded trigger hits as lines spanning the duration of your

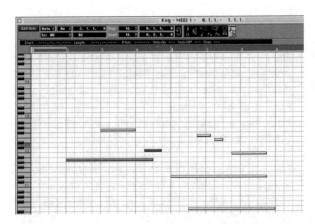

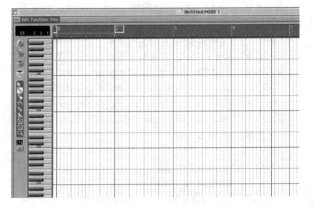

Logic Matrix Edit window (above) and Cubase Key Edit
window (below). Editing in either is fundamentally the same

performance, each of which lines will correspond to a note on a keyboard, displayed on the left of the Key Edit page. Remember, if you're editing a particular part that's situated within your track, you'll only see the material you wish to edit if your part is highlighted, which you do by clicking on it or by glueing all parts associated with your track together, which isn't always the best option.

The Key Edit grid is divided up into beats and bars along its horizontal axis and notes (as seen on a regular keyboard) on its horizontal axis, and there is a bar running across the top of the Key Edit window that shows you the duration of the part you're currently editing. The Snap dialog box allows you to change the look of the main grid, according to the subdivision you're editing within, and the Quantise dialog box allows you to move notes to any groove setting you choose. All velocity, modulation and pitch-bend information is displayed on a controller display running along the top of the Key Edit window, underneath the Quantise dialog box.

Tools In Key Edit

Using the toolbox, you can edit individual MIDI hits. (This differs from working in the main Arrange page, where you're editing whole parts.)

These are the main functions of each of the tools that you will find in the Key Edit window:

Pencil

The Pencil tool enables you to draw new pieces of trigger information into your created part and reduce or increase the duration of your existing material. By using the Pencil tool, you can also create and manipulate controller data.

Eraser

The Eraser tool serves the same purpose in this editor that it does in the main Arrange page – you can use it either to delete single hits or to erase a number of trigger hits simultaneously by drawing around them.

Paintbrush

This tool is extremely useful in drum programming, whether you're working in Drum Edit or Key Edit mode. If you line up the Paintbrush tool next to a particular note and draw a straight line directly across for the required duration (measured in bars), the notes will automatically snap to the quantise setting highlighted at the top of the editor, and in the Individual Quantise function, that applies to that particular note. The Paintbrush tool can also be used to program runs of trigger hits, such as hi-hat lines and snare fills.

Pointer

The pointer tool is used for editing and moving recorded trigger information within the editing grid. Where the information is moved to is dependent on the quantise setting you choose within the editor. If you choose a 16th-note quantise setting, your information will move only to a 16th-note subdivision of a bar. For example, if you were programming a fast drum roll which needed a faster resolution of notes to achieve the desired result, you'd have to change the subdivision in the drop-down Quantise dialog box in the Key Edit window. The Pointer tool can also be used to highlight single or multiple notes for copying – hold down the Pointer tool holding down the ALT key (PC) and drag the copy to its new location within the editor. Notes can also be deleted by selecting a single note or holding down the mouse button and drawing around the recorded information and pressing the Backspace key on the keyboard.

Crosshairs

The Crosshairs tool allows you to manipulate controller data in the Controller Information bar, which runs along the bottom of the Key Edit window. Using the Crosshairs tool, you can globally increase the level of your data – for example, globally increasing the velocity of snare-drum hits situated within a part. It can also be used to smoothly fade in and fade out controller data, and if you've ever heard that slowly fading in machine-gun roll on a dance record, you'll be aware of what the tool can do. To use it, select a position within the grid, depress the mouse button and drag the Crosshairs tool along the controller information bar. All trigger information within the capture range will be affected.

Kicker

The Kicker tool can be used to move recorded trigger information one subdivision to the left or right of the editing grid. In fact, this is a pretty useless tool, and once again the information is moved in steps defined by the quantise value that has been chosen.

Speaker

Dragging the Speaker icon over your recorded information will allow you to reference individual trigger hits.

Drum Edit (Cubase)

In Drum Edit mode, all of your recorded drum hits are shown as diamonds situated within a grid, which tells you which particular drum sound is being triggered and where it is situated within the bar. The image over the page shows a typical Drum Edit window.

basic Rhythm Programming

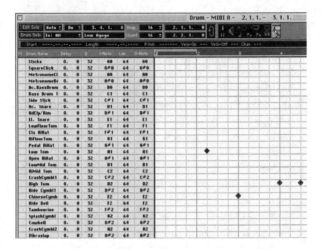

Cubase Drum Edit window showing recorded drum hits

Provided that you've set your Track Class to Drum Track, you can enter into Drum Edit by double-clicking on your information block situated on the main Arrange page. Instead of a keyboard running down the left-hand side of the editor, you'll see a drum map telling you what drum sounds you have access to and which MIDI note you're sending trigger information to in your sound module.

In Drum Edit mode, drum maps can be customised and

saved as .drm files. The most common drum map is known as a *General MIDI drum map*, which has global default settings for all the major elements of a drum kit such as bass drums, hi-hats, snare drums and toms, and this drum information is a collection of different sounds mapped across the keyboard as opposed to one single sound tuned chromatically across the keyboard. The Drum Edit toolbox is slightly different from that used in the main Arrange page or Key Edit window, and you'll also find that each drum sound will have not only its own mapping but also its own quantise setting.

HiFloorTom	0.	0	32	61	64	61						
Pedal HiHat	0.	0	16	6#1	64	6#1						
Low Tom	0.	0	32	A1	64	A1						◆
Open HiHat	0.	0	16	A#1	64	A#1						
LowMid Tom	0.	0	32	B1	64	B1						
HiMid Tom	0.	0	32	C2	64	C2						
CrashCymbl1	0.	0	8	C#2	64	C#2						
High Tom	0	0	32	D2	64	D2						

Segment of the Cubase Drum Edit window showing individual quantise settings

The toolbox for the Drum Edit window is identical to the one that is used for Key Edit, with the exception that you'll need to use the Drumstick tool to enter in new information. The Drumstick tool can also be used to erase single drum notes.

Controller Information

At this point in the proceedings, it's worth introducing you to the concept of *controller information*. MIDI is very much a multi-faceted form of data communication and has a far greater capability than just the recording and playback of trigger hits on a grid. Later on in the book, I'll be getting into the specifics of manipulating controller data in relation to particular rhythmic patterns, but we can make an initial start by accessing the main controller display, which is common to both Key Edit and Drum Edit windows in Cubase VST.

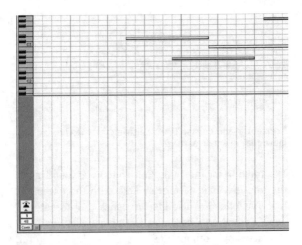

Controller display and default controller indicator

On the bottom-left-hand corner of your edit page, you'll see an arrow. Clicking on this will bring up a Controller display, and above the arrow you'll see a Controller icon. Basic controller data could be defined as a device that enables you to transmit performance-related MIDI events, which can then be recorded by your sequencer. MIDI controllers are normally keyboards. Examples of controller data are Note On and Note Off messages and pitch bend, modulation and velocity information. MIDI controller information can also be assigned to specific parameters within your synthesiser. A modern sequencing package will give you the ability to record and edit MIDI controller data.

The most important thing to remember about controller data is that, by definition, controller data needs something to control. If there is nothing to control, then no matter how many controller hit points you program into your Controller display, you'll hear no difference in your MIDI recording. Controller data can be used to control many parameters, such as pitch bend, modulation, velocity, panning, breath control and sustain, which are just some of the default settings available to you – there are many more assignable controllers that can directly affect any programmable feature within an external or internal synth. Here are a few examples to explain the use of controller messages in more detail.

Velocity

The easiest controller to obtain a direct result with little effort is the Velocity Controller. To access the Velocity Controller, click on the arrow on the bottom-left-hand corner of your edit page and select the velocity icon from the list that appears. The Controller display bar will be filled with velocity hits, which you can manipulate singly by using the Pencil tool or globally

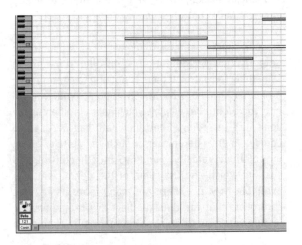

Controller display showing Velocity Controller settings

by using the Crosshairs. When you're in Drum Edit mode in Cubase, you'll only see controller information once you've clicked and highlighted a particular drum voice text box (situated to the left of your editing grid).

Pitch Bend

If you click on the controller icon again and choose the Pitch Bend icon from your Controller dialog box, a new, blank Controller display will appear. Not only can you run multiple controllers at the same time, you can also can draw in controller data by holding down the Alt key and using the Pencil tool. If you press Record, you can also program controller data in real time as your track plays.

Using Controller Data

Due to the fact that controller messages are transmitted through MIDI, you'll need to run a MIDI out from your keyboard into your sequencer. Where it goes then, of course, is entirely up to you – using your Output column, you can send the data to an external synth or back to your keyboard (if it contains sounds).

The easiest way to understand the concept of controller data is to say that any movement of a knob and any program change can be recorded into your sequencer and then edited in your Controller menu. Controllers that are common to every controller keyboard or module – such as pitch bend and modulation – will already have default settings assigned to them and be visible in the initial Controller menu. However the amount of controller assignments is vast, and they all work on a number basis. If you explore the edit pages of your external module, you will find that there are default numbers assigned to each particular parameter within your external module or internal instrument. These numbers can be changed, but for the purposes of this example you should leave them alone.

Examples of these controller parameters are resonance, movement (which makes the sound move between speakers), attack and decay. When changing any of these parameters, remember that you're applying this to a particular sound on the MIDI channel you've selected. Not only that but you're applying your editing to a particular block of information on your edit page, which may last for only a couple of bars.

Once you've found the controller numbers assigned to the various parameters for the module that you wish to control, the next step is to assign them to an edit page in your sequencer's Controller sub-menu. Taking Cubase as an example, as you scroll down the Controller sub-menu you will see an 'Other' option:

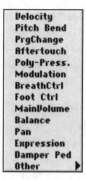

Cubase controller sub-menu

Clicking on this while holding down the mouse will bring up a list of numbers. If the resonance filter on your external synth is set to default 15, choose the number 15 on the list. This will bring up a blank Controller 15 edit box. If you're recording in real time, any movement of the controller knob on your module will be logged on that particular edit screen, and the data can then be manipulated with the Pencil tool.

Controller messages are an invaluable aspect of programming and will provide an essential missing link to any drum programming you embark upon. However, it's essential to remember that, when using sequencers, you have to be in control of your time-keeping; it's great to make a groove sound lazy or edgy, even if it happens by accident, but this will make your programming life hell if you haven't followed a simple rule and lined up your beat 1 with your sequencer's beat 1.

The way in which I'm describing the use of controller data here lends itself to three distinct methods of programming:

- Programming in two-, four- or eight-bar chunks. Imagine the hassle of programming and editing a 30-bar drum loop. I'm all for rambling filter sweeps, but be careful!

- Separate your drums into individual tracks. You may want to apply a resonant filter to your hi-hat but leave your snare and bass drum well alone. Working on the Drum Edit page in Cubase will allow you to treat each drum voice separately, although it won't be easy to arrange your drums if they're housed within the same part.

- Ghost parts are definitely the way to go, initially, as trying to replicate detailed groove and controller editing to bar upon bar of groove can be an extremely time-consuming process. When you copy a single part by holding down the Ctrl key on the computer keyboard, this will turn everything you copy into a ghost part. For bulk copying, go to the Structure menu, select 'Repeat Parts' and then 'Ghost Parts'. Every edit applied to the main master part will be reflected in the ghost copy.

Soft Synths And VST Instruments

As well as the sounds housed within external keyboards and external sound modules, you'll also have access to internal sound modules known as *soft synths*. A soft synth is a virtual synthesiser housed within your soundcard and can be accessed in the same way as an external synth from the Output menu on the main Arrange page of your sequencer. Individual sounds can be chosen from the instrument panel in the Inspector, situated to the left of the main Arrange page.

A further soft-synth development is instruments that are described as being native to a particular software sequencing package, and one such example is the group of soft synths known as *VST instruments*. These are soft synths that can be accessed within your software package. New VST instruments are being developed all the time, and the sounds they produce are generally pretty good and certainly worth including in your timbral palette.

Tutorial 1: Assigning VST Instruments In Cubase

1 Choose a MIDI track by highlighting it with the computer mouse.

2 Go to the panels on the main Cubase toolbar and select 'VST Instruments' from the main drop-down menu.

3 Choose the virtual synth that you want to use from the drop-down list that appears.

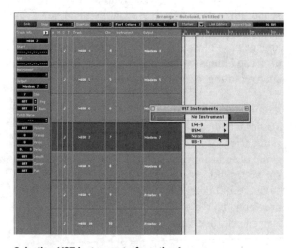

Selecting VST instruments from the Arrange page

4   Go to the main Output dialog box, situated to the right of your MIDI track, and choose the synth you wish to output to.

5   Choose the sound you require from the Instrument panel in the Inspector.

The advantage of native instruments is that no setup is required, and you can normally edit sounds onscreen.

Saving

If you're happy with what you've done, at this point it's worth saving your file. When you first click on your application icon (red diamond for Cubase, blue circular motif for Logic Audio), the Arrange page that you see will be an autoload or 'def.all', which is a default Arrange page. The def.all file will already have default settings programmed in by the manufacturer, including such things as screen size and magnification, track layout and Track Class listings, all of which can be changed to suit your needs. By the time you've completed your initial MIDI recording, you will have customised this default page to some degree.

If you save your file without first renaming it, you will have altered your default Arrange page, which can be extremely annoying because then, every time you start a new arrangement, you'll have to spend time resetting your main Arrange page. Obviously, you can customise your Arrange page, but be careful which settings you choose to appear as defaults every time you start a new arrangement – for example, you might wish to keep certain outputs, but you might want all of your tracks unnamed so that, if you decide to use a different palette of instruments from your previous arrangement, you don't have to waste time erasing names in order to rename them again.

To save your files effectively, it's prudent to rename your file. This is done by going to the File menu (situated on the main toolbar) and selecting 'Save As', which will bring up a dialog box giving you the option of renaming your file and choosing a folder for it.

Following this procedure will enable you to access your files with ease. There's nothing more frustrating than having files scattered all over your hard drive in no relevant order. A useful tip is to save all of your files in one global folder called, for example, 'Grooves' and creating within it sub-folders named by musical genre. By following this procedure, you can easily access a default Arrange page by clicking on the main Cubase diamond icon or you can quickly access grooves itemised by genre, which can save an incredible amount of time and energy. Accessing files in this way means that you're merely fine-tuning existing grooves and sounds to suit a particular arrangement rather than starting from scratch each time. As I mentioned earlier, nearly all musical genres will have their own common tempos, sounds, programming and arrangement techniques that set them apart from other musical genres, so having a genre catalogue is invaluable.

All sequencing packages will also let you save information in a number of different formats, which are denoted by the extension attributed to the file name, as shown here, with the definitions of these formats listed below:

.ALL

If you save a file in this format, you're creating a song file. Song files are the most extensive type of file, as they not only include information relating to your particular arrangement but also every piece of information relating to your application, including all of the files associated with your application, all recorded audio files and even general preferences.

.ARR

This stands for *arrangement* and will save all data pertaining to the arrangement on which you're working.

basic Rhythm Programming

However, there are some segments of data that it omits on the audio side, such as that used by the Audio Pool (an audio-file management system relating to a particular arrangement). You'll find that .ARR files are most commonly used when it comes to saving exclusively MIDI material.

.PRT

This suffix stands for *part* and relates to a particular part contained within an arrangement or a group of parts. Parts are chosen by first highlighting them and then saving. Once again, the ultimate destination folder is determined by the user.

.MID

This is a very commonly used file format for communicating with other MIDI sequencers and samplers. A .MID (MIDI) file contains MIDI track information, and there are two types of MIDI file format: Type o and Type 1, with the former containing one track that plays back on any MIDI channel and the latter containing the original track structure contained within an arrangement. To save your MIDI information as a .MID file, go to the File menu in the Cubase toolbar and select 'Export MIDI File'. This will call up a dialog box asking you if you want to save your file as a Type o or Type 1 MIDI file, and it will give you the opportunity to name your file for future reference. You can also input a MIDI file into your arrangement by selecting 'Import MIDI File' in the Import sub-menu in the File menu. The imported MIDI file will then be imported straight into your arrangement and butted up against the left locator.

.WAV, .AIFF, .MP3 And SDII

These are audio file formats. The first, .WAV, is an audio-file format used on PCs, although .AIFF and .MP3 can be read by both Cubase and Logic Audio. Meanwhile, .AIFF and SDII files are Mac-format files.

2 MUSICALITY AND MUSIC THEORY

In order to achieve effective grooves and not leave everything to chance, it's important to grasp the concept of how beats are divided and how drum grooves are formulated.

The important thing to remember about MIDI programming is that it's an extremely creative way of working. Later on in the book, I'll be looking at audio recording and beat creation in depth, but unless you're a drummer yourself, you'll be predominantly working with audio samples and you'll be reliant on working with pre-recorded audio loops from sample CDs that have been used many times before. Obviously, you can overcome this if you're prepared to trawl through records to find new and interesting beats, which is a valid way of doing things, or if you know a drummer who is prepared indulge you in a sampling session. The best approach, without a doubt, is to combine resources and have a good working knowledge of both media.

When you're programming MIDI drums, you'll mainly

be dealing with single samples, unless you're triggering whole drum loops via a MIDI sampler (which will be looked at later on). This method of drum programming requires you to be able to dissect a rhythm and recreate it, adding your own rhythmic slant and drum samples. To understand exactly what drum programming involves, it's worth taking some time to discuss the properties of a traditional acoustic kit and see how traditional drum voices are applied to the creation of programmed drum grooves.

The bass drum on a modern drum set provides the bottom end to a groove. However, the degree of emphasis it has on the foundation and make-up of a rhythm is totally dependent on the genre within which you're working. For example, a rock groove will rely on the bass drum and snare to provide body and direction – the bass drum will either lock in directly with the bass line or maintain a constant pulse, enabling the bass and the other instruments to weave in and out,, creating rhythmic contrast. In rock, the snare drum provides a backbeat and interacts with the bass drum, creating a two-voice anchor for the rhythm section. Both voices are extremely dynamic, and the way in which they interact together dramatically affects the shape and feel of a rhythm. At the other end of the spectrum, if you're working in a jazz idiom, the main

pulse of your groove will be provided by the ride cymbal and the hi-hats, while the bass drum and snare will weave in and out of the main pulse, reacting to melodic phrases created by the other instruments.

Drum Voices
Hi-Hat

For those of you who aren't familiar with a traditional drum set, here is a short explanation of what a hi-hat actually is. On a traditional drum set, the hi-hat can be played in an open or closed position or in any number of countless divisions between these two basic positions.

A traditional hi-hat constitutes a pair of cymbals that are placed on a stand and operated by a foot pedal, enabling the user to open or close the hi-hats together. Sound is produced by hitting the hi-hats with a stick at the same time as separating the two cymbals via the stand's footplate.

Ride Cymbal

In the context of a traditional drum set, the ride cymbal provides a top-end pulse. Used in its most basic context, a ride cymbal provides the rhythmic glue to push a track forward and creates a platform for the bass drum and snare to subdivide against.

Toms

Toms, which can range from a small 6in top tom to an extremely low 16in or 18in bottom tom, are used to either crochet the backbone of a track (as found on some tribal dance records) or they can be used to create drum fills, which are commonly employed to move from one musical section to another in the context of an arrangement.

Crash Cymbals

Crash cymbals are used to highlight and punctuate musical phrases. The metal is far thinner than the ride cymbal, so they're louder and have more overtones. Crash cymbals come in a range of sizes, from splashes (normally 6in or 8in) to full-bodied crashes (normally 16in or 18in in diameter). They are again in the top register of drum set's voices, along with the ride cymbal and hi-hats.

The best thing to do in a programming situation is to trust your ears when it comes to picking exactly which crash to use. Crash cymbals would normally be heard in conjunction with a drum fill and effectively put a full stop to the end of a phrase. They can also be used to mark the start of sections, and in some cases they can be played in the same manner as a ride cymbal, giving a driving rhythmic pulse to a tune. You can place a

bass-drum hit underneath a crash cymbal to give added weight to the phrase you're highlighting.

Of course, there's a difference between playing the drums and drum programming; the programming traits and techniques associated with computer-generated rhythms can be exceptionally challenging in terms of the co-ordination and technique used to recreate them on an acoustic drum set. The most interesting evolution that has occurred as drum programming has progressed is that, in order to create rhythmic tension within an arrangement, most new forms of music have rearranged the way in which drums are perceived within a musical piece. For instance, as a drummer, before I started programming drums, when I played a song I would always play a fill to bridge into a new section – for example, from a verse to a chorus. This would draw the listener's attention to the fact that a change was going to happen and would aid in resolving a musical section (which basically means drawing one section in a particular arrangement to a close and starting a new one).

While this approach is still widely used and indeed a totally valid approach when programming in many genres of music, many programmers who are making music may have never played a drum kit in their lives, giving them a totally new approach to the instrument.

Instead of recognising a sample as a bass drum or snare, they will simply hear it as a low sound or a mid-range sound, therefore discarding the drumming constraints of playing a bass drum and snare drum in the traditionally expected way. Many programmers, particularly those working with newer forms of music, will create tension in an arrangement by doing the reverse of what a traditional drummer would do – for example, instead of filling into a section, many programmers will totally cut out certain elements of the drums from the arrangement, such as the bass drum and snare, to bring tension and dynamics into a song.

Looking at things from a drumming perspective, in my opinion all drummers should always be ready to change the way in which they hit the drum set in order to achieve the sound they want. For instance, in order to get the required sound for a particular groove, a drummer may be required to dig the drum stick into the snare to achieve a dull, muted sound, while another groove may require a perfectly executed double-stroke roll. The sound you're making is the important factor. If a drummer confines himself to a particular grip or bass-drum technique, he's greatly limiting the choice of drum sounds and feel that he can apply to a piece of music. The same view should also be adopted when it comes to drum programming – if you end up using

a sub-bass sound for a bass drum in preference of a traditional-sounding bass drum, so be it. As we move further into our programming styles during the course of the book, I'll be showing you how to combine many different sounds to create rhythmic tension and flow.

Above all, the most important thing about being a musician is maintaining an open mind. The fact that many of the people who are involved in and learning drum programming aren't drummers is, in my opinion, a good thing. Music is always evolving and has no rules in either its inception or its delivery. People will make music with whatever resources are available to them. Whether you've studied your chosen instrument for years or you've just bought a new computer and have no formal music training at all, whatever you create musically should be considered valid and should be judged only by whether it communicates with people. What is important now more than ever is to remember that, when you're programming drums, you should keep things simple and look for textures and sounds. It doesn't matter if the voice you're planning to use for a bass-drum figure doesn't resemble the sound of a traditional bass drum; if it works within the arrangement, then it works.

What's becoming more and more apparent as the

creation of music with the use of computers progresses is that musicians who use this medium are treating rhythm with a lot more freedom. Musicians, particularly those involved in the newer cutting-edge styles, have no rules with regard to the physical limitations of reproducing a rhythmic pattern live or which sounds should be used to play the role of a particular drum; sounds are blended together until the collective noise is deemed good by the user.

Having good technique, co-ordination and motion doesn't necessarily make you a good drummer – some of the most renowned drummers have no technique or knowledge of different styles to speak of, but the one thing they *do* all have in common is a great feel and sound, even if it's limited to the music performed by their chosen band. A record either feels great or it doesn't – you can't see how someone holds their sticks by looking at a CD player.

Later in the book, I'll be showing you how to create rhythms for a number of different musical genres by using MIDI- and audio-programming techniques, but for now, to get us started, I'm going to dissect a basic rock rhythm and recreate it using a MIDI sequencer. First, though, let's look at the drum voicing of a basic rock groove.

A drum kit is basically a collection of a number of different voices which, when played in a certain order, create a groove. The elements of a drum set that supply the tempo and drive to a musical arrangement are the bass drum, hi-hats, snare drum and ride cymbal. This isn't to say that rhythms can't be created from any sound at all, but it pays to keep things simple initially. To program our basic groove, we'll use three elements of our drum set: the bass drum, hi-hats and snare drum.

Within the MIDI domain, sequencers basically work in the same way as the traditional method of recording, except that, instead of having to study for years in order to physically articulate a drum groove, you have a selection of single drum samples that you have to assemble. Initially, you'll be looking at these three voices and working within your sequencer's default time signature of 4/4, with a tempo of 120bpm (beats per minute). Let's put our MIDI sequencer into Record Ready.

Fast-Track Cubase Recording Guide

1   First, make sure that you're sending and receiving MIDI information and that your MIDI Thru is activated and you're sending and receiving MIDI.

2   Set your click. If you double-click on the Click icon,

this will bring you into the Click Setup dialog box. Leave the click set to the default precount length of two bars. If you're working in a time signature other than 4/4, you'll need your click to reflect this in order for your recording to make sense.

3 For the purposes of this exercise, use the default tempo of 120bpm.

4 Choose the appropriate quantise setting, depending on the note subdivision you're using.

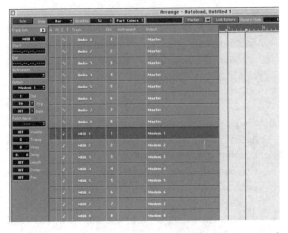

Cubase Arrange page showing tracks, channels, output and track class

5   Select a track to record onto by clicking on it with
    the mouse, then click on it again to name it. Once
    you've named the track, press the Return key on
    the computer keyboard. (The track name will
    translate to the parts created on that track.)

6   Select the class of track you require by pulling
    down the Track Class menu in the Arrange page
    and selecting what type of track you want your
    recording to be, using the mouse. (The Track Class
    column is located in the main Arrange page and
    marked 'C'.)

7   Choose a MIDI channel. By now, you should be
    communicating with either an external sound
    module, the sounds situated within a soundcard
    or a native instrument. (Drums are set to default
    MIDI channel 10.)

8   Check your controller keyboard. You should have
    access to sounds that you will be hearing either
    through your soundcard's Line Out socket or from
    the output of an external module connected to
    your mixer.

9   Set the positions of your locator to a length of
    one bar.

10 Activate the click by pressing the Click icon (situated on the Transport bar) with a mouse click.

11 Choose Overdub or Replace mode. As I mentioned earlier in the book, when your sequencer is set to Overdub, your new MIDI hits will be added to your previously recorded MIDI information as you continue to record on the same track. In Replace mode, on the other hand, new MIDI data will overwrite all of the previously recorded information on that track. For the purposes of this initial exercise, we will use Overdub mode. (One extremely useful exercise for programming drums is to master the art of counting out loud.)

12 Activate your sequencer, by pressing Play with the mouse. The sequencer's default click setting will be quarter notes, and your MIDI click will be set to trigger a voice (normally a rimshot or a cow bell), which will have a default of MIDI channel 10 and a note of C1. Listen to it and start to count out loud in groups of four: 'one, two, three, four', and again, 'one, two, three, four', making sure that your vocalisation is in time with that of the click. Continue this for a minute or two, then press Stop on the sequencer and return your position indicator to the start of beat 1.

Note Values

While this book is not intended to be a music-theory text, it's worth taking some time at this point to understand how the use of note values and note placement are crucial to effective drum programming.

Subdivision is probably one of the most important concepts to grasp when it comes to drums, whether you're physically playing them or programming rhythms. In the West, most popular music is written in a time signature of 4/4, and in this system of subdivision the upper figure determines how many beats there are to a bar and the lower note gives you their value. For example, 4/4 means that there are four quarter notes (crotchets) in each bar. These quarter notes can then be equally divided into a number of subdivisions, depending on how fast or slow you want your resolution to be. When programming, the speed of your drums is also dependent on the bpm (beats per minute) you choose. As an example of how these two settings interact, if you choose a time signature of 4/4 and a bpm of 60, you've made the decision that each bar of music will be defined by four equal quarter-note subdivisions, just like you were cutting a whole cake representing one bar of music into four equal segments. Also, because you've chosen a tempo of 60bpm, each of those beats will take one second (ie

1/60 of a minute) to pass, so four beats will be heard in four seconds. Therefore, the tempo you choose will determine how much time your drum groove will take to complete one bar and the subdivision (ie the time signature) will determine the resolution of the notes played during that period. Here are some typical subdivisions of bars:

1   Eighth notes, where eight equal beats pass in the time it takes to complete one bar.

2   12th notes, where 12 equal beats pass in the time it takes to complete one bar.

3   16th notes, where 16 equal beats pass in the time it takes to complete one bar.

4   24th notes, where 24 equal beats pass in the time it takes to complete one bar.

5   32nd notes, where 32 equal beats pass in the time it takes to complete one bar.

You should be able to see that, although the tempo has stayed constant, the amount of notes you're able to play within the allotted tempo or time frame has changed. This is in short how the Quantise function works. Once you've chosen your quantise setting, the sequencer will automatically snap the events in an arrangement to the subdivision you've chosen. This can be done either before the recording process has begun or after you have completed it. The advantage of using the Quantise facility after you have completed your recording is that, by playing freestyle without a chosen quantise subdivision, you can move freely between subdivision settings without having the sequencer get in the way. However, you can end up in a bit of a mess if you're not careful, so it's usually best to decide your upper subdivision limit (ie the length of each beat) before you start recording. I normally choose a 16th-note setting initially, changing to a new quantise setting at any point during the recording process if I want to play faster.

Start off by programming a pattern whereby the bass drum plays on beats 1 and 3 in your counting process and your snare drum plays on beats 2 and 4. Start your sequencer again, and this time, instead of counting 'one, two, three, four', change your vocalisation to bass, snare, bass, snare', once again counting in time to the sequencer's quarter-note click pulse. You may feel a little stupid doing this, but believe me, this concept is at the very heart of the drum-programming process.

1   Set your left and right locator positions to a one-bar cycle and turn your sequencer's Loop function on. Now, when you press Play, your sequencer should cycle over a one-bar pattern. Once it reaches the start of bar 2, it should immediately loop back to the start of bar 1.

2   Now match your count with the numbers that appear on the top bar counter of your main Arrange page. Your bass drum should match with beats 1 and 3 and your snare with beats 2 and 4 over one bar of time. When you reach the end of the bar, stop the sequencer and return it to the beginning of bar 1.

3   Go to your MIDI keyboard and find your bass-drum and snare samples. If you're using a General MIDI drum map, you'll find your bass-drum sample on C1 and your snare drum on D1.

4   Start the sequencer and again match your count with the numbers on the top bar counter, but this time through hit the bass-drum and snare-drum keys on your keyboard in time as you vocalise 'bass, snare, bass, snare'. When you've completed this stage of the proceedings, you're ready to commit to a MIDI recording.

Recording

When you press the Record button on the Transport bar, the sequencer will give you a precount click as a default and the recording will take place from the left locator's position. As soon as the recording has started, you can play your information into the sequencer. Depending on the record mode that you've chosen, the sequencer will either stop recording as soon as it hits the left locator (Punch Out) or it will continue to cycle between the right and left locator positions (Cycle Record).

Once the recording is complete, press the Stop icon, rewind your song position indicator back to the left locator (using the Rewind button on the Transport bar) and click on the Play icon. (This operation can also be achieved by clicking on the Stop button a second time, which will also return your song position pointer to the left locator's position.) By pressing Play on your sequencer's Transport bar, you'll be able to listen back to your recording as the MIDI information you've recorded (represented as a block of information on the main Arrange page and situated between your locator positions) is retriggered by your sequencer.

Quantising

This is the point where the term *quantise* really starts to make sense. If you've been reasonably accurate in your playing, the quantise setting on your sequencer will automatically snap your bass-drum and snare beats to exactly match the click track as the sequencer cycles around its one-bar loop. If you're hearing a disparity between the quarter-note click and your bass-drum and snare beats (which, incidentally, are also quarter notes), you have made an error that the sequencer hasn't been able to deal with. At this point, if you're not satisfied with your recording, you can delete it by pressing the Backspace key on the computer keyboard. However, if you want to rectify what you've done, you have to select the relevant block of information and open up an editor. You can open editors in two ways:

- Double-click on the block of recorded information you wish to change and you will automatically be brought into an editor.

- Go to the main Toolbar and choose 'Edit' from the edit drop-down menu or use a key command. (Default key commands are situated to the right of the main drop-down dialog strip on the main Toolbar.)

When you open up the editor, you'll see the grid shown over the page. In Cubase, If you haven't specified a drumstick icon in your Track Class strip in the main Arrange page, you'll automatically open the Key Edit window.

basic Rhythm Programming

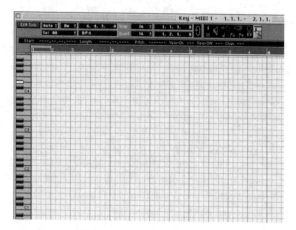

Cubase Key Edit window

When you're in the editor, set your main quantise and snap functions. The subdivision that you choose will depend on how much faster the notes you've been playing are than a quarter note.

To choose between editors in Logic Audio, go to the Windows drop-down menu situated in the main Toolbar. The most user-friendly editor in Logic is the Matrix Editor, which has a similar look to the Cubase Key Edit window. It's basically a grid representing divisions of a bar of music where your recorded information is

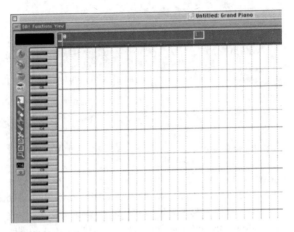

Logic Matrix Editor

shown as strips. If you've set your quantise time before you started recording, all of the strips aligned to the actual notes you played on your keyboard will have automatically snapped to the beginning of each beat – the bass drum will be lined up exactly with beats 1 and 3 and your snare will fall exactly on beats 2 and 4. However, if they're out of alignment then you have two choices:

- Leave the note-trigger strips alone and continue on with the rest of your recording.

basic Rhythm Programming

- Quantise the recorded information so it lines up exactly with beats 1, 2, 3 and 4 on your grid, which will in turn totally synchronise your recording with your click track.

In this exercise, we're going to follow the second option and quantise our recorded information.

The easiest way to quantise your MIDI information in Logic is to select all the recorded information within your editor by drawing around it with the pointer tool and clicking on the Q icon situated to the left of the matrix editor – this will cause all of your information to snap to the nearest chosen subdivision. For instance, choosing an eighth-note quantise setting from the drop-down quantise list in your Matrix Edit window will instruct the sequencer to ignore any notes played outside the eighth-note catchment area. In other words, any information you played that was faster than an eighth note will disappear and the sequencer will automatically snap everything you do to the nearest eighth note. In this instance, we could easily get away with a quantise setting of 4, which would snap all of our played notes to a quarter note. Remember that, once you understand the theory of what applying quantise to your recorded information does, you'll be able to apply this to any sequencing package. Also remember that all of your recorded information will play back independently of any other recorded MIDI information, as long as it's been assigned to a different MIDI channel.

Now let's move onto our first interactive tutorial and record the next part of our drum pattern. The third voice we're going to use will be a hi-hat, a pair of cymbals that along with the ride cymbal articulates the top end of a groove. It's also one of the most expressive voices and forms the heartbeat of almost all computer music grooves. As we get more into the specifics of programming for different music genres, I'll be talking about the tone and texture of your drum voices, but for now use a basic hi-hat sound, which will be on MIDI channel 10 and with General MIDI default of F1.

Our basic hi-hat pattern will be programmed in an eighth-note subdivision, which is basically doubling the initial quarter-note bass-drum-and-snare groove.

Tutorial 2: Creating A Basic Hi-Hat Pulse

1 Using the same loop points as you used in the previous exercise, select another track on the main Arrange page.

basic Rhythm Programming

2   Change the MIDI channel of your new track to channel 10. Bear in mind that a drum patch will have different drum sounds mapped to different notes across the keyboard, so you won't have to change MIDI channels in order to program in a new drum sound.

3   Name your track by double-clicking on the Track Name column.

4   Return your sequencer to the start of your loop position and press Play.

5   As the sequencer plays back your previously recorded information, count out loud 'one-and-two-and-three-and-four-and'. The previous count of 'one, two, three, four' should directly coincide with the bass, snare, bass, snare, just as it did before, but now in between each count you should articulate a count of 'and' – in effect, directly doubling the speed of your count.

6   Make sure that your quantise setting on the main Arrange page is to eighth notes or above.

7   Locate your hi-hat sample on your computer keyboard.

8 Press Record on the sequencer's main Transport bar, as you did before.

9 As soon as the two-bar precount has elapsed, start recording. (Remember that you're doubling the speed of your click pulse.)

10 Once you've completed your one-bar cycle, stop your sequencer.

11 Listen back to your recording and decide whether you need to quantise it. The hi-hat part should be falling exactly on beats 1, 2, 3 and 4 and should be evenly spaced throughout the bar.

12 If you need to tighten up your part, double-click on the block representing your hi-hat information and open up your editing window. You won't see your bass-drum or snare parts there because they're on different tracks, but you will see your recorded hi-hat pulses.

13 Set the quantise value to 8 in the Quantise dialog box in your editing window and once again choose the Q function on the main Arrange page or in the Matrix Editor. Once the information has been quantised, you should have a perfect one-bar MIDI

drum loop. The loop actually sounds fairly familiar and is an extremely good vehicle to help you grasp the concept of what drum programming is actually all about.

Rhythmic Contrast

If you've chosen a quantise setting of 16th notes, your sequencer will accept notes of anything up to and including that value. All rhythms are basically constructed by offsetting different note values against each other, and drum programming is no exception. To turn a group of drum hits into a groove that has direction and rhythmic contrast, one voice will move in steps of one subdivision (note value) and another voice will move in a different, contrasting value. This is the very essence of rhythm, which creates interest for the listener.

Another thing to observe is the inclusion of *rests* – in other words, areas where notes in a rhythm are missed out. If we didn't include rests, all we'd be doing would be playing lines of different subdivisions and layering them across each other. For example, if you programmed in a line of eighth notes to form the basis of a hi-hat part, the interest in the rhythm would come from how the other programmed voices wove in and out the constant hi-hat line. If your snare-drum line was programmed using a resolution of 16th notes, you wouldn't have to play every note – you could leave gaps in your recording, which would make your groove push and pull against the even hi-hat feel. The same can be applied to your bass-drum programming.

Tutorial 3: Broken Snare And Bass Pattern

Let's program our next groove using eighth-note and 16th-note quantise settings, inputting these settings as below.

1   Use the same recording setup as before, but this time start with our basic eighth-note hi-hat pulse and a slightly slower tempo (70bpm).

2   Using the same loop points, select another track on the main Arrange page and change the MIDI channel of your new track to channel 10. Name your track by double-clicking on the Track Name column, then return your sequencer to the start of your loop position and press Play. As the sequencer plays back your previously recorded information, count out loud 'one-and-two-and-three-and-four'.

3   Ensure that the quantise setting on the Arrange page is to eighth notes or above.

basic Rhythm Programming

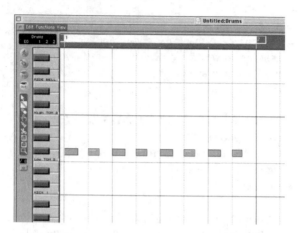

Quantised hi-hat pattern in Logic Audio's Matrix Editor

4   Locate your hi-hat sample on your computer keyboard.

5   Press Record on the sequencer's main Transport bar.

6   As soon as the two-bar precount has elapsed, start recording.

7   Once you've completed your one-bar cycle, stop your sequencer. Listen back to your recording and

decide whether you need to quantise it. If you need to tighten up your part, double-click on your hi-hat information block, just as you did before, and move into your editing window. Set the quantise value to 8 in the Quantise dialog box and once again choose the Q function on the main Arrange page or in the Matrix Editor.

This time, we'll be recording the bass-drum and snare-drum parts onto the same track, so you'll see all of your parts together within the editor window and they'll appear on the main Arrange page as one single block of information. What we're about to do now may sound a little strange at first, but bear with me – it does work and it will give you an idea of how you can very easily structure a rhythm.

8   Return to the main Arrange page and set your quantise value to 16th notes. Return your sequencer to the start of your loop position and press Play. As the sequencer plays back your previously recorded information, count out loud 'one-e-and-a-two-e-and-a-three-e-and-a-four-e-and-a'. Here, what you're doing is doubling again the speed of your count, increasing your subdivisions to 16th notes. (Bear in mind that the tempo hasn't changed, only the amount of notes that you're fitting into your chosen time frame.) The

'one' and the 'and' will exactly match your recorded bass/snare and hi-hat pulses, and the 'e' and the 'a' will fit exactly between these beats. The same, of course, will be true for beats 2, 3 and 4 – you're now counting in 16th notes and you'll have 16 evenly spaced beats within one bar.

9   Make sure your quantise value on the main Arrange page is set to 16th notes.

10 Locate your snare-drum sample on your computer keyboard.

11 Press Record on the sequencer's main Transport bar. As soon as the two-bar precount has elapsed, start recording. While counting out loud, hit the snare on all four 16th-note subdivisions of each beat.

12 Once you've completed your one-bar cycle, stop your sequencer. Listen back to your recording and decide whether or not you need to quantise it. Again, if you need to tighten up your part, double-click on your information block on the main Arrange page and move into the editing window.

13 Set your quantise to 16th notes in the Quantise dialog box in your editing window and once again

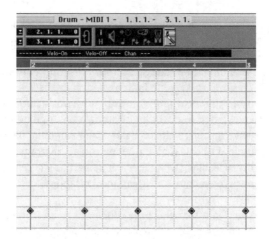

Cubase Key Edit window showing 16th-note subdivisions

choose the Q function on the main Arrange page
or in the Matrix Editor. Repeat exactly the same
process for your 16th-note bass-drum part.

What you've recorded won't be of any musical worth
yet, but what we're going to do now is edit this line
and clear some space within the groove. This is an
extremely simple way of creating an interesting and
dynamic groove. When you press Play, what you
should have is an exactly matched bass-drum and
snare-drum line, with the hi-hat joining on the first

and third hits of every beat. Now let's carry on with the tutorial.

14 Assuming that you're still within your editing window, go to your Toolbox and grab the Eraser tool. This is where you draw on your acquired knowledge from the first tutorial. We're going to leave the snare hits on beats 2 and 4 and the bass drum on beats 1 and 3 during the editing process because, along with our hi-hat pulse, this will centre our groove into something recognisable.

15 You'll see that the bass-drum, snare and hi-hat beats are on three separate lines. What you have to do next is randomly rub out a selection of bass and snare beats, leaving the key hits covering the four beats in place.

This procedure can be done in two ways. If you leave the sequencer running and erase notes as you loop your one-bar cycle, this is called *real-time programming*. If you decide to stop the sequencer and erase notes and then play over your corrected pattern to check out what you've done, this is known as programming in *step time*.

Here's an example to give you an idea of note placement.

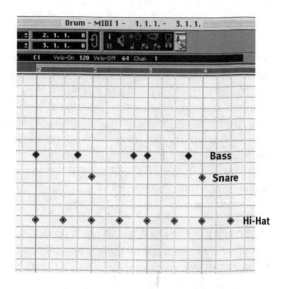

Cubase Drum Editor showing bass, snare and hi-hat hits

However, the best way of creating interesting rhythms is through experimentation and trial and error.

Note how the cleared space allows the groove to breathe. This method of formulating grooves is a very good way to start programming. So far we've used three of the most widely used subdivisions: quarter notes, eighth notes and 16th notes. For the next set of tutorials, we're going to be working in groups of three and six, traditionally known as *eighth-note triplets* and *16th-note triplets* respectively. These two subdivisions are widely used and are known as 8T and 16T respectively when programming in Cubase or Logic. You'll also see subdivision and quantise settings written as divisions of a bar, such as '12th notes', indicating that there are four sets of triplets to a bar (ie three eighth notes to each quarter-note pulse), and '24th notes', indicating that there are four sets of 16th-note triplets to each quarter-note pulse. Let's repeat the previous tutorial and apply it to 12th notes and 24th notes.

Tutorial 4: Eighth-Note Triplets

1   Using the same one-bar loop points, select another track on the main Arrange page and mute your previously recorded material.

2   Change the MIDI channel of your new track to channel 10 and rename it, then return your sequencer to the start of your loop position and press Play, making sure your click is activated. As the sequencer plays back, count out loud 'one-two-three, two-two-three, three-two-three, four-two-three'. You're now subdividing your quarter-note pulse into four equal groups of three. Again, your count will be referencing each quarter-note pulse during your one-bar loop

3 Make sure that your quantise value on the main
   Arrange page is set to eighth-note triplets (8T) or
   above.

4 Locate your hi-hat sample on your computer
   keyboard, then press Record. As soon as the two-
   bar precount has elapsed, start recording. Play all
   12 notes, allotting three notes to each quarter-note
   pulse.

5 Once you've completed your one-bar cycle, stop
   your sequencer. Listen back to the recording you've

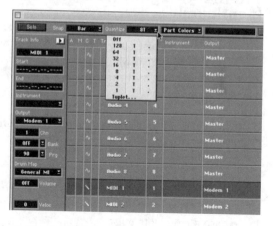

Cubase Quantise options

just made and decide whether or not you need to quantise it. If you think you do, double-click on your hi-hat information block and move into your editing window. Set your quantise to 8T in the Quantise dialog box and, once again, choose the Q function on the main Arrange page or in the Matrix Editor (Logic).

The bass drum will be played on 1 and 3 in your counting process and your snare drum will play on 2 and 4.

Tutorial 5: Eighth-Note Triplets (Continued)

This time, we're going to break up the bass-drum and snare-drum lines and use our grid to help us with note positions. We'll be starting with our basic hi-hat pattern again, so return to the main Arrange page and set your quantise value to 8T.

1   Locate your hi-hat sample on your computer keyboard.

2   Return your sequencer to the start of your loop position and start recording after the two-bar precount. Play all 12 notes, allotting three notes to each quarter-note pulse.

3 Once you've completed your one-bar cycle, stop
   your sequencer, listen back to your recording and
   decide whether or not you need to quantise it. If
   you think you do, access your Quantise function
   in the usual way (see previous tutorials) and set
   the value to 8T.

Okay, let's stay in the editor. You should see your
quantised hi-hat line on the screen in front of you.
We're now going to program in step time, which as
I've explained previously is inputting notes when the
sequencer is stopped. Our bass-drum and snare hits
are going to be punched in manually, using the
Drumstick tool.

One of the advantages of Cubase is that it does have
a specific Drum Edit page, which is a great deal clearer
than most other editors when it comes to programming
drums. On this page, all of your drum hits are marked
as icons and can be rubbed out or punched in using
the Drumstick tool, situated in the Drum Edit window's
own toolbox. Also, the Drum Editor doesn't show you
the duration of your notes – ie how long you held
your finger on each note – and so your edit window
isn't cluttered with different-sized strips of information.
Drum sounds are nothing more than short, single
samples, and to simplify matters Cubase represents

drum information as diamond-shaped icons that change in shading depending on how hard each key was hit during the recording process.

But now back to the tutorial...

4   To start with, punch in your bass-drum and snare-drum hits to give the rhythm a sense of direction. Play the bass drum on beats 1 and 3 of the bar and your snare drum on beats 2 and 4 of the bar. Remember that, when recording eighth-note triplets, your bar is divided into four groups of three and your bass drum and snare are marking the first beat in every division of three. Your hi-hat will still be playing in a '*one*-two-three, *two*-two-three, *three*-two-three, *four*-two-three' rhythm. (Make sure you set your Snap value to 8T to see the appropriate scale.)

5   Now punch in additional bass-drum hits on the 'three' of the first beat and the 'three' of the second beat.

6   Punch in an additional snare-drum hit on the 'three' of the fourth beat.

7   Press Play on the Transport bar and listen to the result.

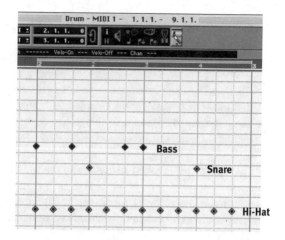

Cubase Drum Editor showing bass, snare and hi-hat hits

Try out combinations of bass-drum and snare-drum hits, such as in the screenshot above.

Tutorial 6: Triplet Patterns

This time you're going to break up the hi-hat and the bass and snare lines, keeping the tempo fairly slow at 70bpm. Our basic hi-hat pattern will play on the 1 and 3 of each beat, while the quantise setting remains 8T.

1   First of all, set up your one-bar loop as before and start recording hi-hat pulses. Record for the whole

bar, but leave out the second beat in each group
of three (ie play the hi-hat on hits 1 and 3 of each
'one-two-three' quarter-note pulse).

2   Once you've completed your one-bar cycle, stop
and play back what you've recorded, checking to
see if you need to quantise things (using the 8T
setting, as before).

This type of rhythm is called a *shuffle*, and the fact that
you've left out the second hi-hat beat in each group of
three will give the groove a consistent disjointed feel.
This is an extremely common rhythm and is used often
in blues.

3   We're now going to program in step time again, so
stop the sequencer and open the Drum Edit window.

We'll be using the same basic pattern, with the bass
drum on beats 1 and 3 and the snare on beats 2
and 4. Remember that your bar is divided into four
groups of three and your bass drum and snare are
marking the first beat in every division of three.

4   Punch in your additional bass-drum hits on the
'three' of the first beat and on the 'three' of the
third beat.

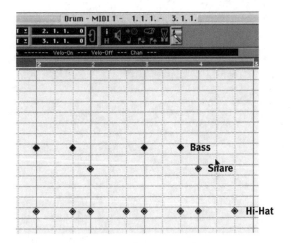

Cubase Drum Editor showing bass, snare and hi-hats

5   Punch in an additional snare-drum hit on the 'three'
    of the second beat and the 'three' of the fourth
    beat.

6   Press Play on the Transport bar and listen to the
    result.

As before, try out different combinations of bass-drum
and snare-drum hits. There's an example at the top of
the next page.

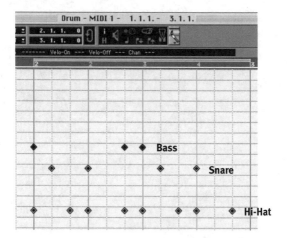

Cubase Drum Editor showing bass, snare and hi-hat hits

Tutorial 7: Triplet Patterns (Continued)

This time we're going to elongate the bass-drum and snare-drum note positions and create a half-time shuffle feel. We'll still keep the broken hi-hat feel and the tempo will remain constant at 70bpm, with the quantise set to 8T and the same basic shuffle hi-hat pattern remaining constant throughout the bar.

1 First of all, set up the hi-hat shuffle as described above. (Refer to the previous tutorial if you've

forgotten how to do this or you've lost your data.)
Call up the editing window if you need to quantise.

2   Take a look at the quantised hi-hat line that's in
    front of you. We're going to be programming in step
    time once again, so your sequencer should be
    stopped.

Once again, we'll be working from the same basic
pattern that we looked at earlier, but because we're
recording a half-time feel, our basic backbeat bass-
drum/snare-drum pattern will contain half as many
notes. The other note placements will again weave in
and out of our basic feel. The bass drum won't play on
beats 1 and 3 of the bar and the snare drum won't play
on beats 2 and 4 of the bar; instead the bass drum
will play only on the first triplet note of beat 1 and the
snare drum will play only on the first triplet note of
beat 3.

These note placements have effectively halved the time,
although it's a rhythmic illusion because the tempo has
remained constant.

This is a classic half-time shuffle rhythm. By halving
the backbeat, we've totally changed the feel of the
rhythm that we've created. The additional bass-drum

hits will occur on the three of the first beat and the three of the second and fourth beats. The additional snare-drum hit will be on the two of the first beat.

You can obviously try any combination of bass-drum and snare-drum hits with the half-time shuffle rhythm, but remember that the main thing that distinguishes the groove from a full shuffle is the placement of the snare and bass drum. As soon as you over-use the snare, the feel will disappear.

Here's an alternative half-time-shuffle arrangement:

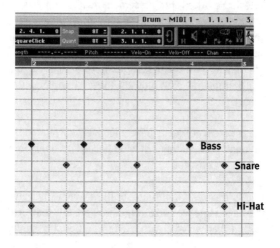

Tutorial 8: 16th-Note Triplets

This time we're going to break up the hi-hat/bass/snare lines, but we'll be keeping the tempo constant at 70bpm. The quantise setting will now move to 16T, giving us three more possible note positions within our grid.

1   Return your sequencer to the start of your loop and, after the two-bar precount, start recording. This time, the hi-hat pattern is the same triplet-note rhythm as the previous exercise, but the basic resolution has increased, so there's more room for error.

2   Record for the whole bar but leave out the second beat in each group of three. Instead, play on just 1 and 3 for each quarter-note pulse, as before.

3   Once you've completed your one-bar cycle, stop, listen back and decide whether you need to quantise. If so, double-click on the hi-hat block, as before, to open the editing window. Set your quantise to 16T.

4   Take a look at your quantised hi-hat line. If you notice a discrepancy in the pattern, all that's happened is that, when your notes were quantised, the increased resolution enabled the computer to place your hi-hat beats to the nearest 16th note,

so any minor mistakes may have been pushed to a different area within the editing grid. To rectify this, click on the note you wish to move with your Pointer tool and drag it to the desired position within the grid. (The 16T resolution means that you've split up each of your four quarter notes into six equal parts.) Your shuffle hi-hat pattern should fall on the first and fourth segment of each beat.

We'll be working from the same basic pattern here, but again, because we're recording a half-time feel, our basic backbeat bass-and-snare pattern will contain half as many notes. Remember that the

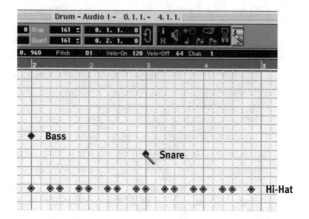

other note placements will again weave in and out of the basic pattern. The bass drum won't play on beats 1 and 3 and the snare drum won't play on beats 2 and 4. Instead, the bass drum will play only on the first triplet note of beat 1 and the snare will play only on the first triplet note of beat 3. These note placements have effectively halved the time, although it's a rhythmic illusion because the tempo has remained constant. Remember that your bar is divided into four groups of six, with the bass drum marking beat 1 of your first group of six and beat 1 of your third group of six, with the snare marking the first beats in the second and fourth groups.

5   We're editing in step time again, so select the Drumstick tool (Logic Pencil tool).

6   Punch in your additional bass-drum hits on the 'four' of the first beat, on the 'four' of the third beat and on the 'six' of the fourth beat.

7   Punch in an additional snare-drum hit on the 'one' of the second beat, the 'six' of the second beat and the 'two' of the third beat. Remember that you've already programmed in your default pattern, so here you're simply supplementing that basic pattern.

8   Press play on the Transport bar and listen to the
    result.

Again, you should try different combinations of bass-
drum and snare-drum hits, such as that shown in the
example here:

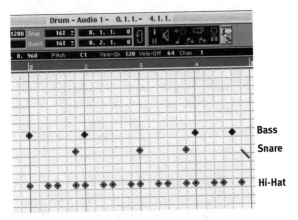

Tutorial 9: 16th-Note Hi-Hat Pattern

In this tutorial, we're coming out of 12th-note and 24th-
note triplet resolutions and going back to a more even
feel. The tempo is going to remain constant at 70bpm,
and this time the quantise setting will be on 16 in the
main Arrange page. (This will take back your sequencer's

correction facility to straight 16th notes, dividing each of your beats into four equal segments.)

1   First off, select a new track to record on and mute your other material.

2   Make sure you're set to MIDI channel 10.

3   The hi-hat pattern you'll be recording will cover all four segments of your four quarter-note pulses. This time, your count will again be 'one-e-and-a-two-e-and-a-three-e-and-a-four-e-and-a'.

4   Once you've recorded a complete one-bar cycle, stop your sequencer, listen back and decide whether you need to quantise things.

5   Open up your editing window and set the quantise value to 16 in the Quantise dialog box.

6   You should see your quantised hi-hat line in front of you. We're going to program in step time again, so the sequencer will be stopped.

7   Again, we'll be working from a basic pattern, with the bass drum playing on beats 1 and 3 and the snare on beats 2 and 4, as shown over the page.

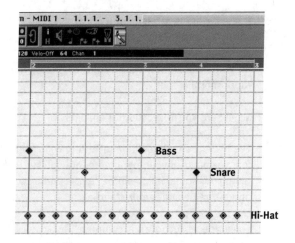

This rhythm is rather reminiscent of our very first pattern, except that the hi-hat pattern has changed.

Once you've keyed in the basic pattern, you'll see that the bass, snare and hi-hat beats are on three separate lines, as before. We're now going to randomly insert bass-drum and snare hits within our 16 hi-hat pulses, leaving the key beats covering the four-beat rhythm already in place.

Try this procedure in real time. Leave the sequencer running, make sure it's in Cycle Record mode and press

Record. This process can be done in either the Drum Edit window or in the main Arrange page, although working in the editor window will give you a greater sense of what you're doing because you can see the notes being entered as you hit the bass drum and snare drum on the keyboard.

If you make a mistake while recording in real time in the Drum Edit window, you don't have to stop recording. Just go to the toolbox, select the Eraser tool, erase the offending trigger hit and continue adding to your drum program. This can all be done without hitting the Stop button once. (Remember that, in order to program in real time effectively, you should make sure that you're in Overdub mode, otherwise every time the sequencer returns to the beginning of its cycle it will erase your previously recorded information.)

Tutorial 10: Broken Hi-Hats

In all of the tutorials so far, the hi-hats have been kept constant while the bass and snare patterns have provided the rhythmic contrast. This time we're going to break up the hi-hat line by leaving out the second hi-hat pulse in every group of four. The quantise value will be set to 16 in the main Arrange page – this will take back your sequencer's correction facility to straight 16th notes, dividing each of your beats into four equal segments.

basic Rhythm Programming

1 Select a new track to record on, mute and switch to MIDI channel 10.

2 Return your sequencer to the start of your loop position and start recording your hi-hats. This time, the hi-hat pattern will miss out the second hit of your four quarter-note pulses. Your count will remain 'one-e-and-a-*two*-e-and-a-*three*-e-and-a-*four*-e-and-a', but this time miss out each 'e' and instead play the 'one' and the 'and-a'. Keep all of your spacing equal.

3 Once you've completed your one-bar cycle, stop your sequencer and listen back to the recording that you've made. You should have 12 equally spaced hi-hat pulses.

4 Decide whether you need to quantise it. Open up the editing window and set the quantise value to 16.

5 We'll be recording in step time again, working with the same basic pattern. The bass drum will be played on beats 1 and 3 of the bar and your snare drum will be played on beats 2 and 4.

6 You'll see that the bass-drum, snare and hi-hat beats are on three separate lines, as before. Now randomly insert bass-drum and snare hits within the 16 hi-

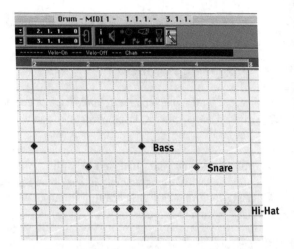

hat pulses, leaving the key beats covering the four quarter notes in place, as shown above.

Tutorial 11: Broken Hi-Hats (Continued)

For this exercise, the tempo will remain at a constant 7obpm and the quantise will be 16.

1   Select a new track, mute your previously recorded material and select MIDI channel 10.

2   Return to the start of your loop and start recording.

basic Rhythm Programming

Again, the hi-hat pattern we're going to record will cover all four segments of your four quarter-note pulses. Your count will be 'one-e-and-a-two-e-and-a-three-e-and-a-four-e-and-a'.

3 Record for the whole bar. You should have 16 equally spaced hi-hat pulses. Listen back and quantise if necessary.

4 You should see your quantised hi-hat line in front of you. We'll be programming in step time again, using the Drumstick or Pencil tool to punch in the basic bass and snare parts.

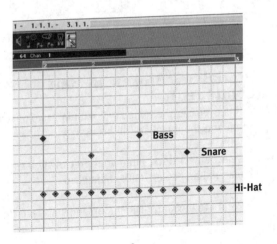

5 This time, we'll be removing hi-hat hits from the 16 hi-hat pulses. This can be done in either real time or step time. The number of notes that you remove is totally up to you – the more gaps in the pulse, the more disjointed the rhythm will feel.

On the previous page is an example of the above tutorial to give you an idea of hi-hat note placement.

Tutorial 12: Broken 16th-Note Bass, Hi-Hat And Snare

For this exercise, keep your quantise setting at 16 in the main Arrange page.

1 Select a new track (set to channel 10) and mute all of your others.

2 Return your sequencer to the start of your loop position and record four groups of four hi-hat hits, as before.

3 Listen back to your recording and decide whether you need to quantise it. If so, set the value to 16.

4 You should see your quantised hi-hat line in front of you. In step time again, randomly remove hi-hat hits from the 16 pulses, just as you did in the

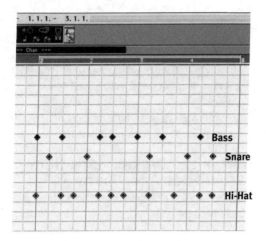

previous exercise. Use the same 1-and-3 and 2-and-4 bass/snare-drum pattern.

5   Once you've done this, in real time randomly insert additional bass and snare hits within the 16 hi-hat pulses, leaving the key beats covering the four quarter notes in place. Leave the sequencer running, make sure it's in Cycle and Overdub mode on the Transport bar and press Record. As I said earlier, this procedure can be performed in either the Drum Edit (Matrix Editor Logic Audio) window or on the main Arrange page.

An example of this kind of pattern appears at the top of the previous page.

Accents

Accents are of great importance when it comes to making a rhythm flow. They're normally applied to single drum hits to create rhythmic interest. When we speak, we accent certain words we want to draw attention to, and we also conclude sentences with a pause. The same kind of thing applies to rhythms increasing and decreasing the velocity of various notes within a groove will add interest to the rhythms and help you add feel to your programming. Every time you record material into your sequencer using a MIDI play-input module, such as a keyboard, the sequencer records not only what notes you hit but how hard you hit them. When you open your editor, you will be able to see this *velocity information* in a number of ways. These velocities can be edited by using your sequencer's Velocity Controller.

Tutorial 13: 16th-Note Running Hi-Hats

This exercise requires you to record a 16th-note running hi-hat pattern and apply velocity changes to it. The quantise setting will be 16 in the main Arrange page, which will take back your sequencer's correction facility to straight 16th notes, dividing each of your beats into four equal segments.

1   Select a new track to record on, mute everything else and set your new track to record on MIDI channel 10. Again, find your hi-hat sample on your keyboard.

2   Return your sequencer to the start of your loop position and press Record on your Transport bar. Again, the hi-hat pattern you're about to record should cover all four segments of your four quarter-note pulses. Your count-in will be 'one-e-and-a-two-e-and-a-three-e-and-a-four-e-and-a'.

3   Once you've completed your one-bar cycle, stop your sequencer, listen to your recording and decide whether you need to quantise it. If so, double-click on your hi-hat information block and move into your Drum Edit window.

4   Set your quantise to 16 in the Quantise dialog box.

5   You should now see your quantised hi-hat line in front of you. You will be programming the next passage in step time, so your sequencer will be stopped.

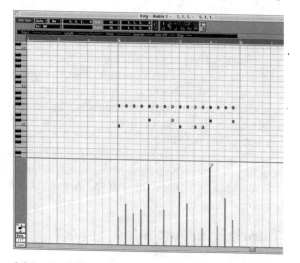

Cubase Key Editor showing hi-hat, bass-drum and snare velocities

6   On the bottom-left-hand side of the Cubase editing window, you will see an arrow. To access the Velocity Controller, click on the arrow and select the Velocity icon from the list that appears. The controller display bar will fill with velocity hits that you can manipulate singly by using the Pencil tool or globally by using the Crosshairs.

7   When you're in Drum Edit within Cubase, you will

only see your controller information once you've clicked and highlighted a particular Drum Voice text box, situated to the left of your editing grid. Do this now and randomly change the velocities of your recorded material by clicking on your chosen hit in the controller display with your Drumstick tool and pulling the Velocity volume up or down. (This action can be applied to all MIDI trigger information.)

Your hi-hat pattern should now have a totally different feel. The changes in the velocity of your hi-hat hits will give your recording an ebb and flow.

Tutorial 14: Accented Snares

For this exercise, the quantise value will again be set to 16.

1   Select a new track (set to MIDI channel 10) and mute all of your previously recorded material.

2   Return to the beginning of your sequencer loop and press Record, then lay down a hi-hat pattern that covers all four parts of your quarter-note pulses.

3   Once you've recorded the entire sequence, listen back to your recording and decide whether you need to quantise it. If so, double-click on the block

of information in the usual way. You should see your quantised hi-hat line in front of you.

4   Programming in step time again, first punch in some bass-drum hits on beats 1 and 3 and snare-drum hits on beats 2 and 4. Now insert additional bass and snare hits within the 16 hi-hat pulses, leaving the four key quarter-note beats in place.

5   Now use the Pencil or the Drumstick tool to insert a snare-drum hit on the fourth 16th-note segment of the second quarter note and on the second 16th note of the third quarter note.

6   Now insert a bass-drum hit on the third 16th-note segment of the first quarter note and on the third 16th-note segment of the third quarter note.

7   Match the volume of the snare hits on the second and fourth quarter notes, giving them a value of 120. This is done by clicking on the Velocity Controller strip with either the Drumstick tool or the Pencil tool, depending on which Cubase editor you're in. The volume will be shown in the Velocity Controller window situated above the Velocity Controller icon in the bottom-left-hand corner of the Cubase Drum or Key Edit windows.

8 Decrease the value of all the other snares to a volume of 70.

9 Give all of the bass-drum hits an equal volume of 120.

10 Return the sequencer to the start of bar 1 and press Play.

Performing this procedure makes the main snare hits accented and leaves the underlying snare-drum hits unaccented. These unaccented notes could also be described as *ghost notes*.

By using your Controller Editor, you can manipulate a number of controllers in this way. All of the controllers will work independently of each other. The Velocity Controller is the easiest controller to start with and is directly applicable to drums. We will be using other controller data manipulation later on when the grooves become genre-specific.

3 AUDIO RECORDING 1

As computer power has increased, it has become possible to integrate real audio into recordings and record real sounds such as bass, drums, guitar and vocals along with MIDI information, which, you'll remember, is a series of trigger hits sent via your sequencer's output path to trigger a sound module.

When you record audio into your computer, you're converting real sounds – such as a drum kit being played by a drummer in real time – into digital information, which is then stored on your computer's hard drive as an audio file. There are three things to consider when you're about to embark on the audio side of the drum-programming process:

1   How do you get audio into your computer?

2   How do you listen back to it?

3   Once you've recorded it, how can you manipulate it and make it a useful part of your recording?

basic Rhythm Programming

Three very important questions. But first I think it would be useful to get a little background into why it's so essential to record and manipulate audio drums when, by the use of MIDI, it's now possible to trigger countless samples from a vast array of modules and synthesisers. To answer this question I'm going to use just one word: *feel*. All musicians will have a way of playing a piece of music or a groove that's particular to them. I'm not saying that everyone who plays a live instrument is good, but when you record a piece of audio you're essentially taking a snapshot of one particular moment in time.

The term *feel* can be used to sum up a number of different aspects of a rhythm. It could be the fact that the timing of a groove wavers ever so slightly, enabling the rhythm to move and sit better with previously recorded material. There may be background noise on a recording that gives a groove a non-clinical feeling to it. Basically, what you'll find, either through listening to other people's recordings or through continued development of your MIDI skills, is that the use of audio will expand your drum-programming palette enormously.

When I use the term *recording audio* I don't want you to confuse this with manipulating pre-recorded samples and loops that are available on countless CD-ROMs. I'll be looking at this concept later in the book, when I'll be giving you some tips on how to create new audio material cheaply and effectively. To achieve this, however, you'll have to be resourceful in your choice of venue and to become familiar with the recording side of your sequencing package.

The process of recording audio doesn't have to be expensive, and believe me, it will be extremely rewarding. At this point, some of you will probably be saying, 'That's all very well, but I can't play drums.' My solution to that would be to put up an advert in any rehearsal room and give a drummer a job (they'll probably do it for free, anyway). The advantage of doing this is obvious: you'll have the opportunity to record drumming that's totally particular to you and your own personal recordings. Obviously, not all forms of music require drums that have a human feel; some genres, such as dance, rely on the mechanical feel of electronic drum samples, which is totally fair enough, but being articulate in the art of your sequencer's record-input path is essential.

If you happen to be a drummer, my advice is to get your audio-recording and -manipulation skills sorted. The way in which records are being made is constantly changing, and these days many songwriters and producers who are primarily responsible for the creation of records are working in a very different environment from the conventional recording studio. Indeed, studios with live rooms are almost a thing of the past. Today, most records are put together in bedroom-sized studios that are cheap and easy to maintain. Therefore, for the art of drumming to survive and keep moving forward, it's essential that drummers embrace all ways of creating rhythms and using their skills.

One way of achieving this is by working within the new environment used and understood by the new breed of musician, songwriter and producer. You've got your work cut out if you're trying to persuade a songwriter or producer to go into a recording studio at a fee of between £250 and £1,500 ($385 and $2,300) per day so that he or she can record your live drums, but if you take control of the situation and record your own drums using some very simple methods, which I will outline below, you can communicate with the people who are creating music. Remember that music always takes the path of least resistance and embraces all technological advances. Even if the particular musical environment you're working within is a traditional setup, if your recording is going to end up on CD then you're still going to be dealing with the conversion of recorded audio to digital data, so there's really no way to get away from the new studio technology.

Initially, I'll be looking at recording live drums into your computer, something that can be done extremely cheaply. Like I said, recording studios can cost anything from £250 ($385) to £1,500 ($2,300) per day. Now, obviously they will have acoustically treated rooms and state-of-the-art equipment (at least, they should have!), but the problem is that, as soon as you book a studio, the clock is ticking, and if you haven't worked in an environment like a studio before, or if you're working with a drummer that you haven't heard previously, you're taking unnecessary risks. Also, you're totally at the mercy of an engineer who might not have a clue about the type of drum sound you're trying to create. My advice would be to hire a cheap room in which you can make a lot of noise. This will greatly alleviate your time constraints and will give you more time to experiment with mic placement and drum sounds. Rehearsal rooms are always a good option – they're cheap to hire (particularly during weekdays), and if you ask beforehand they'll usually have spare mics that they can lend you. By taking this route, what you're gaining by cutting your overheads is the time to get the grooves and feels you're hearing in your head onto your computer.

So how should you approach recording into a computer? Well, there are two basic decisions to be made:

1   What do you want to record and for how long?

2   How do you physically get audio information into a computer? This will require you to look at the record path and refine your ability to get a good drum sound.

These two questions go hand in hand – after all, there's no point in having some fantastic section of recorded audio sitting on your computer's hard drive if it sounds absolutely terrible and is totally unusable because of an error in the recording process. Similarly, there's no real point in having long-winded, rambling grooves that don't make any musical sense and will take hours of laborious editing to be turned into usable grooves. The best way of discovering what to record is to take a look at exactly what you want to achieve from the recording.

Source Sounds

Your live-drum recording setup can be as simple or as complicated as you wish. Whether you choose to hire a studio or simply rig up some mics in an acoustically flattering room, there will be a certain amount of trial and error involved in the recording process. Every room will have a different natural sound, and it's worth experimenting with various degrees of dampening, both of the room itself and of the acoustic drum set. Drums are extremely live-sounding instruments, and as a general rule you'll be looking for a combination of a natural ambience combined with a degree of separation.

Drum-kit setups and sizes will obviously differ depending on the type of music being played on them and the player's individual preference, but a basic setup comprises a bass drum, a snare drum, two rack toms, a floor tom, a pair of hi-hats, a ride cymbal and two crash cymbals. One of the most important things to remember is that you can put a fantastic mic in front of an instrument and record it, but if your source sound is bad then your recording will also sound bad; the theory of being able to fix it in the mix is a bit of a myth.

Tuning

Let's have a quick look at drum tuning, taking a look at each part of the drum set separately. In order to get the best out of your recording, it's vital that you get a good, clean drum sound. A well-tuned drum set could be defined as one on which each component voice is tuned to the correct frequency range, with a degree of dampening to cut out overtones while still maintaining a resonant natural sound. If a drum has been tuned properly, you should be able to make it fit into any track you're working on with a little manipulation.

basic Rhythm Programming

The tuning of all drums is referred to in terms of turns. By using a tuning key you either tighten or loosen lugs that are situated on the side of the drum. The tighter the drum the higher in pitch, the looser the drum and the lower in pitch. The best way to tune a drum is as follows:

1 Remove the old head by loosening all of the lugs situated around the drum with your tuning key.

2 Get the new head and gently break the glue at the join between the end of the head and the rigid, circular hoop that sits on the drum itself. This process stops the head from stretching and keeps it in tune.

3 Tighten all of the lugs finger-tight, pushing down on the rim of the drum with the palm of your hand to remove any slack. Work diagonally across the head. Remember where you started from!

4 Repeat this procedure on the bottom head.

5 Go back to the top head and, still working diagonally, tighten each lug a quarter-turn.

6 Do the same for the bottom head.

7   Repeat this procedure until you're happy with the sound you're getting. The point of tuning drums this way is that, if both heads are tuned to the same pitch, you're letting the size of the drum do the work for you – there's no way that you can make an 11in tom sound like a 14in floor tom, so if you know that your top and bottom heads are of equal tuning then you're also to experiment with the amount of turns the bottom head has in relation to the top, because you're starting from a level playing field. Also, the thicknesses of the drum heads is a contributing factor to the tuning. The normal rule is that top heads are thicker than bottom heads, with snare heads being extremely thin.

Bass

I'm a firm believer in using old-sounding drums – one of my kits is over 30 years old – but I have to say that the most stunning improvements in drum-kit manufacture in recent years has been the development of great-sounding bass drums that are full of punch and life.

What you're looking for in a bass drum is a degree of top-end click, to add definition, and plenty of bottom-end punch. Traditionally, bass drums have had two heads, but for at least the last 30 years, when recording bass drums, engineers have either had to take off the front head or punch a circular hole in it in order to get a microphone close enough to the rear head of the drum, where the pedal impacts. Bass drums are also normally filled with pillows or some form of dampening material, which serves to cut down overtones and allows for more definition, and they come in different sizes, ranging from 16in in diameter to 26in in diameter. A great bass drum for recording is normally 20in, which will give you enough bottom end but won't be too uncontrollable.

Snare

Some people look at snare-drum tuning and wince. These drums can also come in a range of sizes, from 10in to 14in in diameter, and they also differ in depth, from 3in to 8in. A snare drum has two heads and the bottom head has wires that resonate as the top head of the drum is struck.

Due to the fact that the bottom snare head has wires, it will always be tuned to a greater degree than the top head, normally about a full two turns higher. Dampening can be applied to a snare drum by cutting out a ring from an old snare head using a sharp knife. Start the circle about 1cm ($\frac{1}{2}$in) from the rim of the head and make your ring about 1.5cm ($\frac{3}{4}$in) wide.

When you place this ring on top of the new head, this will dampen the drum evenly. If you find the drum too dead, cut the ring you've made in half and secure half of it to the head of the drum with some gaffer tape.

Toms

Toms can be a nightmare to tune, but if you follow the process outlined at the start of this section you should be fine. Toms have a tendency to ring, which actually isn't a bad thing if your drums are in tune, although if they ring too much you can add a little dampening to the top and bottom heads with some gaffer tape.

Cymbals

Tuning cymbals and hi-hats is very much down to personal taste. The only thing I can say is that you get what you pay for. Obviously, there may be a time when you need a trashy cymbal sound, but on the whole you'll want clarity and definition from your cymbals. Make sure that you choose appropriate crash cymbals for the type of music you're playing, and ensure that your ride cymbal doesn't build up overtones too quickly.

In general, the degree of dampening you use on drums depends greatly on the type of sound you're trying to create, but if they're not in tune they'll *always* sound bad, no matter what you do.

The Recording Process

Depending on the soundcard you're using, you'll have differing degrees of flexibility. Most cheap cards are two-in/two-out devices, which means that anything you record will be recorded into the sequencer as either two mono tracks appearing on two separate tracks on your main Arrange page or as a single stereo pair, representing a stereo snapshot of an audio event on two channels linked together as a pair. As you increase your soundcard budget, you'll find not only that the quality of your analogue-to-digital and digital-to-analogue conversion increases but also that the number of inputs and outputs at your disposal expands.

The first recording we'll be doing will be a straight-for-stereo recording onto a digital recorder, such as a MiniDisc machine. Digital recorders like MiniDiscs are great for hassle-free recording, as they are extremely portable and usually give great results, but the most useful thing about recording with a portable digital recorder is that you can record anything, anywhere, and all of the audio you record into your player can be streamed into your computer at a later date.

The next stage is to stream your recorded information into the recording side of your sequencer. Your soundcard will allow you to connect an output from your MiniDisc player to the input of your soundcard. This can be either a digital connection, which will enable you to transfer your information without any loss of quality whatsoever, or you can use a mini jack connection from the Line Out of your MiniDisc to the Line In connectors at the back of your soundcard.

All rehearsal rooms will have basic mixing desks. The first step is to connect your microphones into the line inputs of the mixing desk and run a line out from the mixing desk into the Line In socket on your MiniDisc player. The Record Level meter on the player will show you if your recording level is too high, although actually arriving at the correct recording level is a method of trial and error, and the sound you get is largely dependent on the positioning of your microphones. One option is to buy microphones specifically for digital recorders, which could be plugged directly into the Line In of the MiniDisc player, allowing you to bypass the external mixer completely.

Microphones

Before getting into microphone setups, it's worth talking a little more about microphone placement. Your choice of microphones and where you place them on your drum set will have a dramatic effect on the sound you're going to get. Depending on what kind of music you're recording and your available budget, there are two types of mics that can be used to record drums. Condenser mics tend to be the more sensitive of the two types and have a high frequency response, which goes up to 20kHz. Some will allow you to change what the mic actually picks up by way of a selector switch situated on the mic casing itself. Three common condenser-mic patterns are:

- Omni (short for *omnidirectional*) pattern, which allows the mic to pick up sounds equally from all directions;

- Cardioid, which allows the mic to pick up sounds mostly from the front.

- Figure of eight, which allows the mic to pick up sounds from the front and the rear but not from the sides.

Condenser mics are normally used to record the top end of a drum kit, such as the cymbals and hi-hats, due to their added frequency response.

Dynamic mics, on the other hand, aren't as sensitive as condenser mics and have a lower frequency response – these are the mics you'll usually find in rehearsal rooms. When using dynamic mics, you have to be in close proximity to the sound source to get any useful level, which is actually fine for drums because they're loud. Dynamic mics can withstand the hammering they get from recording a drum kit very well and are used often on parts of the kit that need to be *close-miked*, such as the toms, snare and bass drum. Bass-drum mics have to be extremely hard-wearing, and they'll also need have to have a good bass response. A classic example of a dynamic mic is the Shure SM58.

When recording drums, depending on the type of sound you're going for, you'll almost definitely be adjusting the type of mic you use and also its placement. For example, you might want to capture the ambience of a room using two overhead condenser mics set up in an omni-pattern setup, in which case the two microphones might be placed either directly over the top of the drums or between 1m (3ft) and 1.5m (5ft) away from the drums, depending on the sound you want to achieve.

The number of mics you'll need to record with will depend greatly on the flexibility of your system and your soundcard's ability to split your recording adequately onto separate audio tracks. If you have a card that can record audio on eight different tracks simultaneously, it's worth close-miking your drum set as described earlier, but if your card is a two-in/two-out model, it's probably best to go for a great natural drum sound.

Remember that the driving elements of a modern drum set are the bass drum, the snare, the hi-hats and the ride cymbal, so make sure that they're all clear and that you're getting enough level into your system.

Drum Frequency Guide

When it comes to EQing your recording, the following guide should help you treat the various parts of your kit sound:

- 5kHz and upwards will represent a drum kit's top end (ie cymbals and hi-hats).

- 500Hz–1kHz will encompass the toms, which will run from an 8in tom to an 18in floor tom.

- 1.6kHz–170Hz will hit the frequency range of a snare drum. If you want to bring out the snares themselves, you should adjust your EQ in the 2–2.5kHz register.

- 80Hz will represent an average bass-drum frequency. If you want to bring out more of the sound of the beater hitting the drum, add more top end to the sound at around 4kHz.

A Brief Word About Effects

As a general rule it's a good idea to leave yourself with as many options as possible, so in this case I would recommend that you record your drums completely dry, without any effects at all, as this will give you a blank canvas on which to work. It's also important to resist the temptation to over-use any effects and EQ parameters that may be available. Ultimately, you may want your grooves to be used by other people to make their own records with, so don't colour your drum grooves with excessive effects or EQ settings that you think are great but will mean that your grooves are unusable by anyone else.

Close-Miking

Below is a typical close-miking setup:

- Bass-drum mic (usually a hard-wearing dynamic) on a small boom stand positioned inside the bass drum.

- Toms close-miked using dynamic mics.

- Snare drum miked using a dynamic mic and placed about 2in above the head of the drum.

- Hi-hats miked using a condenser mic about 2in above the top cymbal and about 1in away from the hi-hat.

- Overhead mics (usually condenser models) placed in a stereo pair above the drum set and positioned to the right and left.

Two-Mic Recording Session

If you have the luxury of recording with condenser mics, you should choose to use cardioid models, which will allow you to pick up sound mostly from the front of the mic. Place a stereo pair on either side of the drum kit, left and right. Make sure you use boom stands for the mics and also make sure that the bottoms of the stands aren't touching any of the kit's hardware stands, as this may lead to noise being picked up during the recording process. You'll still have to engage in a degree of trial and error in order to obtain exactly the right balance you're looking for, but this is still an effective technique.

When you've got the right sound, connect your mics to the inputs of the mixing desk and connect it to the line in of your soundcard, via the Line Out sockets.

Three-Mic Recording Session

This miking technique is known as the *Decca Tree*, after the old Decca studios, and the best mics to use would be condenser models, but these aren't essential. From the centre of the snare, measure three drumstick lengths above the drum and place a mic there, then place the bass-drum mic three drumstick lengths from the centre of the snare. Then place an additional mic the same distance above the floor tom.

Recording Into Your Sequencer

Whether you're recording into your audio package from a mixing desk or you're recording straight into your soundcard, you're basically inputting information into your sequencer, and the path that it follows is called the *input path*. An output is then taken from the mixing desk to the physical line inputs of the soundcard. The signal then passes into your computer's audio mixer. This is the signal's *output path*, and it's at this point that it hits your sequencing package. Once the record inputs have been activated, your signal can be routed to a particular channel and your input signal will appear on your sequencer's internal mixer.

Soundcards And Audio

A soundcard is a piece of hardware that allows you to record real audio into your sequencer, and the quality of your recorded audio is totally dependent on the quality of your soundcard. A soundcard is housed in one of your computer's PCI slots (dedicated slots for accepting cards and extension boards). In order for your soundcard to communicate with your sequencer, it will also require a driver in the same way as your MIDI interface does. As with the MIDI side, a driver is a piece of software that's loaded onto your computer's hard drive and placed in your sequencer's ASIO (Audio Stream Input/Output) folder.

Soundcards vary in their degrees of functionality – some will record only audio and some will contain a MIDI interface and/or soft synths. Those at the cheaper end of the market will enable you to record only left and right in and play back left and right out, whereas if you move to higher price brackets they become more flexible, offering more record inputs and outputs and providing better-quality A-to-D (Analogue-to-Digital) and D-to-A conversion. They also tend to set aside the all-singing, all-dancing approach and just record audio very well, with no MIDI or soft-synth capabilities.

When you record digital audio, you're basically converting your analogue information into a set of numbers, and this process is achieved by the analogue-to-digital converters in your soundcard. The digital information is then stored on your hard drive. To listen back to your recorded information, your soundcard's digital-to-analogue converters change those stored

numbers back to analogue data. The quality of this conversion process is measured by the number of times your soundcard's converters sample the analogue signal, as well as their ability to read the recorded information accurately. Sixteen-bit/44.1kHz sampling is a standard and applies to normal CD quality recordings, and most audio cards will function at this rate. ('44.1kHz' refers to the sample rate per second, while '16-bit' indicates the resolution quality of the samples.) However, there are many other factors that will affect the quality of your recorded audio. It's worth remembering that real audio takes up a great deal of space on your computer's hard drive, so make sure that your computer has enough memory to cope.

All basic soundcards will have a line input to enable you to record audio into your sequencer, and they'll also have a line output, which can be plugged straight into a mixing desk, enabling you to hear recorded audio. They'll also have digital inputs and outputs for streaming in and listening to digital data from MiniDisc players, etc.

However, there may sometimes be problems with recording directly into a soundcard. Some cards don't have balanced inputs, for instance, and they may also not have phantom power, which means that you won't be able to record using high-quality condenser mics.

Software Tutorial: Setting Up To Record Audio

First, make sure that your soundcard has been installed and routed correctly in your sequencer. Go to the ASIO Multimedia Setup panel, where the Input/Output Port lists should show that your card has been selected. Pre-OS X Macintosh users should go to the Sound control panel and check the relevant dialog box.

In order to activate Cubase VST inputs, pull down the Panels menu and select 'VST Inputs'.

Then, in the Options window, select 'Enable Audio'.

On the Status bar at the top of the Arrange page in Cubase, choose 'Enable 24-Bit Recording' (this will only apply if you've installed a soundcard that supports 24-bit recording; normal CD quality is 16-bit/44.1kHz).

Select your sample rate in the Audio System Setup window, then select an audio track by highlighting it

with the Pointer tool. Click on it again to name it. Once you've named the track, press the Return key on the computer keyboard and the track name will translate to the parts created on that track and to the actual audio files created.

Select the class of track you require by pulling down the Track Class menu in the Arrange page. Choose an audio track class (denoted by a waveform).

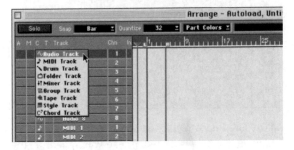

If you're recording in mono and this is your first audio track, select Channel 1.

The Inspector, shown at the top of the next page, indicates the status of your recording. If you want your recording to be in stereo, click on the 'Enable Stereo' icon. Your channel indicator will now be grouped in pairs – ie 1/2, 3/4, etc.

basic Rhythm Programming

Make sure the correct inputs are selected for the audio channel(s) you've selected. These will appear at the bottom of your mixer.

Regular cards will have a stereo-in/stereo-out facility. If you're making a mono recording, select the input to which your sound source is connected. A stereo recording will require different inputs for the two audio channels.

Go back to the Inspector and select 'Record Enable'. This

will make your track and selected audio channel ready for recording. If you're making a track ready for the first time, a dialog box will appear asking you to select a folder in which to store your recorded audio files.

When the Input Meter function is activated, the meter shows the signal level at the input. Be aware, though, that the faders on the internal mixer will have no bearing on the amount of input level that's going into your sequencing package. The amount of input gain can be controlled from the soundcard's dialog box or

Cubase Channel Mixer with function IN to show recording level

from the external mixer. Use the sequencer's mixer faders to adjust the amount of output level.

There are many different ways of recording within Cubase. Personally, I find it useful to define the amount of bars I need before I start.

Once you've finished your recording, press Stop and an image of your recording will be displayed on the Arrange page as a waveform. At this stage, remember to label your wave files correctly; give each file a name that's relevant to its style and type of groove and make sure that you note what speed your file is running at for future reference – for example, 'Fat Hip-Hop 109'.

Hardware Tutorial: Recording Audio

An external mixing desk will enable you to interface with any number of external musical instruments, such as external MIDI modules, record decks and CD players. Anything that's plugged into an input channel of a mixing desk will have the ability to be routed through the desk and either into the input side of your computer's soundcard, for recording purposes, or simply through the desk into an amplifier and then to a set of speakers. (Many speakers are now powered, in which case an external amplifier won't be required.) Also, a mixing desk will allow you to record with a number of microphones. Although many soundcards allow you to connect mics directly to them, often they aren't able to accept the higher-end microphones, as they don't always have balanced line inputs or phantom-power capabilities.

For the purposes of this exercise, we're going to use four microphones, but the same techniques apply when using two or three mics. However, the greater the number of mics you use, the more outputs you need from the mixing desk and the more inputs you need on your soundcard.

1   Arrange the mics around the drum kit.

2   Plug your mics into the inputs on your external mixing desk. If you're using high-quality condenser mics, you'll need to use phantom power, which is found on most studio desks and avoids the need for external mic power supplies. Most mics will also have XLR connectors, providing you with a balanced input.

3   Continue to route the signal through the mixer and into the computer. All studio desks will have a number of outputs called *bus outs*. You can route the four channels (for argument's sake, we'll call them channels 1, 2, 3 and 4) to your mixing desk's bus outs. Of course, the better the desk you've got, the more outputs you'll have, and a standard, cheap

desk will have at least four that are grouped together in pairs – 1/2 and 3/4.

On each channel of your mixing desk you will have the ability to pan. If mic line 1 is the kick mic, then by panning that hard left you'll be assigning that to signal to bus out 1 on your desk. If the snare is being sent to mic line 2, by panning that hard right you'll be sending the signal out of bus out 2. The same applies to outputs 3 and 4.

4   Connect the outputs from your mixing desk to the inputs of your soundcard (assuming that your soundcard has at least four inputs).

5   In the main Arrange page, select four audio tracks and assign then to channels 1, 2, 3 and 4 respectively.

6   Open your main mixer and select inputs 1, 2, 3 and 4 on four separate channels.

You should now see each of your four separate microphones represented on four separate channels in your internal mixer, giving you a far greater degree of separation. Be aware, however, that, if your soundcard has only a two-in/two-out facility, all of your balancing will have to be done by adjusting the input level on the mixer. Your recording can be represented on Cubase's main Arrange page as either a stereo pair or two mono tracks.

Each microphone will plug into an input of your external mixer, which will also allow you to deliver a signal to the computer at a greater line level than the microphone input connections that are found on the backs of some of the cheaper soundcards. Also, an external mixing desk will allow you a great deal of flexibility during the recording process, as everything that's plugged into the desk will have the ability to be routed through the desk's outputs and recorded as audio onto your sequencer.

Remember that the way in which you mix and balance your recorded information can radically alter the sound and feel of what you've played. It's worth bearing in mind the fact that, if your source sounds are poorly recorded, you won't be able to achieve a good drum mix. With this in mind, make sure that you take the time to record your drums to the best of your ability during your recording sessions. As I mentioned earlier, the great thing about rehearsal-room recording is that, if you make mistakes during the recording process, you can easily try again another day for little or no additional cost.

More Recording Tips

- Make sure that you have enough level going into your soundcard.

- Mic placement is critical, so take the time to experiment with positioning your mics during the recording process. Don't assume that you're going to get a great drum sound straight away; it can be extremely annoying to record a series of fantastic takes only to discover that you can't hear the kit properly. Therefore, always record a few bars first to monitor how your drums are sounding before you decide to go for it.

- Try to use the best-quality microphones you can find. Normally, rehearsal-room mics have seen better days, so try a few different ones. Don't just pick the first one out of the box.

- Record your drums as dry as possible. Don't use any effects or equalisation; keep everything as clean and dry-sounding as you can.

- Use your ears. If a groove sounds bad or is out of time, correct it during the recording process. You won't be able to fix it during the mix without an awful lot of time and trouble.

4 AUDIO RECORDING 2

When you've recorded your drum sounds into your sequencer and saved them on your computer (in the folder that you selected during the recording setup process), the next stage is to edit them to your taste. First, though, we should take a look at another way of getting audio onscreen that doesn't involve any recording or miking of live instruments whatsoever.

Importing Audio

As I mentioned earlier, there are countless CD-ROMs available on the market that contain thousands of single drum samples and entire loops that are virtually ready to be loaded straight into an arrangement. The formats of loops and sample CDs do vary, the exact format being determined largely by where you get them from, but they're usually categorised by musical style – for example, hip-hop, drum and bass, etc.

A good CD-ROM will give you a range of single hits and loops, and it should also inform you of the tempo at which each loop runs and contain information indicating whether the loop is a basic pattern or part of a fill. This is usually given in the title of the waveform – for example, 'EX: D&B180 fill' or 'HipHop96 break'. One problem that you may encounter with loops and samples that have been given away for free, however, is that they might be locked files, which means that you can't change them, or they sometimes appear without any waveforms attached to them, which makes editing them almost impossible.

But this is just a small downside – the upside far outweighs this because, by importing audio into any audio-sequencing package, you can have fantastic beats, breaks and sounds at your fingertips and, more importantly, you'll introduce an element of feel into your recording.

To get this audio data into your sequencer, you can import it directly into the main Arrange page by following this procedure:

1   Insert your CD-ROM into the computer's CD-ROM drive. You can then either copy the contents onto your computer's hard drive or work from the information stored on the CD-ROM itself until you find the particular sounds or loops you're looking for. Remember that, once you've chosen a selection

of beats and sounds, you must then copy them onto your computer's hard drive and store them in the same folder as that in which your arrangement is stored. If you don't, your sequencer won't know where to find them. Searching an entire hard drive for errant .WAV files can be a time-consuming experience.

2   Open up your sequencing package. (For the purposes of this tutorial, I'll be looking at how this procedure works in Cubase.)

3   Select an audio track on the main Arrange page by clicking on it with the Pointer tool.

4   Select 'Import Audio' from the File menu and then select the relevant audio folder. The dialog box that springs up will have an Audition button that will allow you to play your samples, and you'll also be given some basic information about the file you're playing, such as whether it's mono or stereo.

5   If you like the sample or loop, click 'Open'. The file will automatically appear on your main Arrange page, on the audio track you've selected.

Alternatively, you can import your audio data into the Cubase Audio Pool (Audio window in Logic) file-management system. The Audio Pool is a log of all of the audio files used in a particular arrangement and contains information such as the names of the files you're using, whether they're mono or stereo, their lengths, sizes and sample rates, the time and date that they were imported into the arrangement and whether they have an image or not. Every cut or edit you make will be logged in the Audio Pool.

To import an audio file into the pool, either press Ctrl + F (PC) or Apple Command + F (Mac) on your computer keyboard or, on the main Cubase Toolbar, select Audio Pool from the Panels menu. Once the pool has been opened, go to the File menu and select 'Import Audio' – you'll see the same dialog box as before appearing in front of you, giving you the chance to audition your loops and samples. Again, select the file you want and it will be imported into the Audio Pool, from where you'll be able to drag and drop it straight into the main Arrange page.

Once you've recorded or imported a piece of audio into your sequencer, it will appear as a block of information on your main Arrange page, and the length of the block will span the duration of the recording. Use the Stop, Start, Fast Forward and Rewind buttons on the Transport bar if you want to listen to what you've recorded.

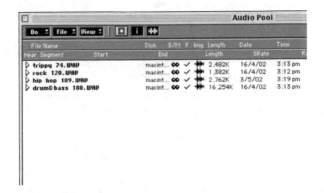

The Cubase Audio Pool

This is where things start to get a little tricky. The difference between recording audio and MIDI is that, when you're using a sequencer to record MIDI, all you're doing is recording trigger information, such as Note On and Note Off messages that tell your internal soft synths or external modules when to play and when to stop. With MIDI, you can change the sequencer's tempo and all of your recorded arrangement will follow suit, and all of the many varied quantise facilities available within Cubase can be employed to correct any wrong notes or timing errors.

Audio, however, is a very different concept. Audio

doesn't have any regard for the tempo at which you're working, unless you've recorded your drums to a click or the loop you've imported is at the same speed (bpm) as your track. If you're working with single samples, your tempo is also irrelevant, due to the fact that they will react exactly the same way as a single bass-drum or snare sample housed within an external module or soft synth.

If you're working with pre-cut and looped samples, you'll have to do little editing to make your drums fit to a track, but you might not be this lucky and the perfect drum loop might be embedded in the middle of a minute of recorded audio drums. The best approach in this instance is to reduce your inspired audio ramblings into bite-sized chunks and make them work at a pre-defined tempo for a number of bars. When the drums you're using are played to an exact bpm and a bar length is applied to them, they can be then used effectively in an arrangement. If you have relatively little editing to do on a drum loop, you can sometimes stay within the main Arrange page, but most of the time you'll be moving between a total of three different audio editors: the Arrange page, the Audio Editor and the Wave Editor. The more accurate editing takes place within the Audio Editor and the Wave Editor.

First of all, we'll have a look at what we can do in the main Arrange page of the sequencer. The format of this page works in the same way for audio data as it does for MIDI information – data is represented as blocks that sit in line with their appropriate tracks and they can be moved around and arranged to your heart's desire. The difference is what is actually housed within the parts. As I said earlier in the book, audio data is just slapped straight onto the main Arrange page, and so, although your blocks of information may look nice and tidy, the audio information contained within them may bear no relevance to the rest of your track whatsoever.

I will remind you at this point that, in order to create individuality in your drum programming, you'll have to broach the other editors at some stage. It's very tempting to work always within the existing tempo and pre-defined bar length of a loop, but it can very quickly get boring and non-creative. The idea is to be able to manipulate your audio files. Even though you might not be a drummer, you should be looking to make all of your audio loops and samples mould your own particular style, and your programming should reflect how you perceive rhythm. This is how a programming style is created. Refer to Chapter 2 for beat-counting exercises.

Rough Cuts

The sequencer's Arrange page is also where you can do all of your rough audio cuts. For example, if you've recorded three minutes of audio drums, it's far easier to work on the main Arrange page and locate the particular segment you require before you move into any of the other editors. You may have decided to record a complete take which lasts the duration of an arrangement, and if the drum take you record is fine, that's all well and good, but you'll often have to perform some editing, either to rectify a mistake or to mould the audio of your track as it changes feel during the writing process.

Drum Looping

The best way of approaching the process of compiling a drum loop is first to listen back to what you've recorded. When you reach a section of your audio material that sounds interesting, stop the sequencer. Drag your right and left locators to the start and end points of your chosen segment and make a cut using the Scissors tool. The audio may not necessarily be starting and ending at pre-defined bar lengths, so the best thing to do is to turn off your Snap function and use your ears to decide where the start and end of your proposed loop is. Remember, this is just a rough cut – the audio can be tided up later.

There are seven things to look for when you're looping a piece of non-defined recorded audio:

1   Consistency of groove. Make sure that the grooves you choose have definite direction and that they have the ability to immediately draw in the listener.

2   Pick your genre. When you're about to embark on a track, it's a good idea to reference material in the same drumming style. That way, you'll recognise a useful groove straight away. If you're a drummer or you're recording a drummer, it's usually better to separate your recording sessions into different styles and save each style in its own named folder on your hard drive, such as 'Hip-Hop', 'Drum And Bass', 'Jazz', etc. This will enable you to reference quickly and exactly a genre from your hard drive instead of trawling through thousands of files. It's extremely frustrating to feel inspired and then spend hours looking for the drum groove you know you have but can't find.

3   A groove will have a start point, which is normally a bass drum. Refer back to the MIDI tutorials earlier in the book pertaining to the shapes of grooves and apply the format to the segments of audio you're trying to locate.

basic Rhythm Programming

4   Within the same audio take, you might find grooves
    that could apply to three or four different tracks,
    so don't discard your audio too easily!

5   If there are two segments of audio that represent
    the same groove and you have to make a choice
    between them, listen for the timing and feel of each
    segment and the quality of the sound. The drummer
    might have played one part of the session more
    level than the other.

6   Make sure that the segment you've selected is in
    time with itself. In other words, you may have
    looped the audio perfectly from end to end, but the
    drummer might have increased the tempo between
    the loop start and end points. It's not the end of
    the world if this happens, but you will need to do
    some pretty serious editing to put it right.

7   You're also looking for drum fills or places where
    the groove might remain the same but the
    drummer's voicing may change – for example, he
    might be playing the same hi-hat-and-snare pattern
    but he could have changed from playing the hi-hat
    to playing the ride cymbal. Depending on the type
    of music you're programming, if you take all of the
    segments of audio that you need for a track from

a particular take, the sound, attitude and overall feel of the drums will be the same throughout the duration of that track.

Once you've done all of this, discard the off-cuts by saving your current arrangement under a different name. This will enable you to clean up your track, erasing any audio-information blocks you know you don't need. The original arrangement will then remain intact and can be referenced easily. You should now be left with lots of different audio sections spanning your arrangement. Assign each section its own track at the beginning of the arrangement and mute them all except for the one you're currently working on.

You can now look to configure your audio segments into a loop so that they can be merged easily into any arrangement. Here are some things to remember:

- A good loop will have to have a consistent tempo from end to end and it will form a repetitive pattern. This will enable you to copy the loop a number of times and formulate an arrangement around it.

- There is no pre-defined number of bars that a loop should be in length, but the longer your loop is, the harder it will be to edit, so you're best off keeping your loops short. If you do have a 16- or 32-bar section that you think is too good to omit from your arrangement, the best thing to do is to chop it into four- or eight-bar chunks, make each piece flow, loop from end to end and save each separate piece as a version of your main master – for example, as 'Groove Master', 'Groove Version 1', 'Groove Fill 1', etc. These three examples will all be bite-sized pieces of your main 'mega' drum groove, meaning that anyone can piece the whole groove together and play it as one complete piece or as inspired individual performances.

If you're a drummer, have a think about this: improving your co-ordination skills will give you the ability to concentrate on exactly how the groove you're playing sounds, as opposed to how you're actually going to play it, and if you define your hand technique, you'll be able to achieve a consistent time feel, which is obviously an invaluable asset.

Audio Editor Tools

Just before we delve into the mysteries of creating loops, here's a brief run-down of the tools found in the Audio Editor's toolbox, where most of the task of loop creation is carried out. You'll find that most of these tools perform similar functions to those found in the toolbox on the main Arrange page.

Pointer
Used to move, highlight or copy audio segments.

Eraser
Used to erase selected audio events.

Pencil
Can be used to import files directly into the Audio Editor. If you click on a lane in the Audio Editor with the Pencil tool, a File dialog box appears. Once you've chosen your audio file, it will appear in the editor.

Scissors
Allow you to cut audio events in the editor.

Mute
Allows you to silence selected audio events within the editor.

Speaker
Allows you to listen to a piece of audio. Hold down the mouse and drag the Speaker tool over the audio file.

Crossfade
Allows you to crossfade smoothly between two audio events. Click on the audio event at the point at which you want the crossfade to start. While holding down

the mouse, drag the Crossfade tool across to the section of audio where you wish the crossfade to end. A crossfade can smoothly join two pieces of audio that are overlapping in some way, and the Crossfade tool seamlessly joins the two segments.

Creating A Drum Loop

The first thing to do with your recorded information is to match it within your sequencer so that it has a defined bar length and tempo. To achieve this, look inside each block of recorded information. You can take any audio segment from the main Arrange page in turn and perform three basic functions on it.

First, you'll have to go into the Audio Editor. You can do this either by double-clicking on a selected audio segment or by going up to the main toolbar and selecting 'Edit' from the Edit menu. Alternatively, press Ctrl + E (PC) or Apple Command + E (Mac).

Once you're inside the editor, you'll see your recorded audio represented as a waveform. You can use the high points in the waveform to assist the editing process – for example, your bass-drum and snare hits will be of a higher level than some other, quieter elements of your recording, and these level increases are mirrored in peaks and troughs in the wave file.

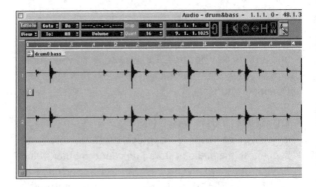

The Cubase Audio Editor

Because you've already cut your audio file roughly in the main Arrange page, you'll only be referencing your chosen segment. The positioning of the segment in the Audio Editor will reflect its position in the main Arrange page, which is shown in the Audio Editor's Song Position strip, located at the top of the editing window, near the main title bar, showing the name of the selected audio track. Close by, you'll see an Information bar, a Functions bar and a Loop function, as well as Quantise and Snap windows.

In the Cubase Audio Editor, you'll see lanes running vertically down the left-hand side of the editing window. These will give you the ability to move your audio information around the editor, which you do by clicking on your waveform with the mouse and dragging your audio to its new position. The way in which your audio moves around the editor is governed by your Snap and Quantise settings.

Editing Your Audio

When you've recorded a piece of audio into your sequencer, the audio is stored on your computer's hard drive. Your sequencer gives you the opportunity to play back the entire audio recording or any portion of it you select from start to finish. When you erase or manipulate a section of audio while working in either the main Arrange page or in the Audio Editor, you haven't permanently erased it – the audio is still stored on your computer's hard drive and all of the cuts you have done are still stored as separate audio segments in the sequencer's Audio Pool. The only thing that has changed is the particular piece of the file you're referencing. The thing to remember is that manipulating and deleting audio from the main Arrange page and the Audio Editor is *non-destructive*, which basically means that, if you accidentally overwrite part of the file you're working on, the data hasn't been irrevocably changed. However, once you manipulate and delete audio information in the Wave Editor, those changes are *destructive* (ie permanent). Also, be careful when using the Cubase Stretch tool, as this also performs destructive editing.

It's worth mentioning at this stage that, if you're working on a particular file that you really like, it's worth backing it up, as some of the features in the Functions menu of both the Audio Editor and the Wave Editor inflict permanent changes to audio files.

When you open the Wave Editor, a wave file will have a start-inset point situated in the top-left-hand corner of the file and an end-inset point situated in the bottom-left-hand corner. These points allow you to increase or decrease the amount of the file you're referencing at any one time. This may sound a little strange at first but it works well.

Audio Cutting

When you make a loop from a non-defined piece of audio, you first have to cut out a section of pre-recorded audio material to use. In this example, I'm using a section of audio that's eight bars long. Here's what you do:

1   Import the audio into the main Arrange page.

2   Using the Scissors tool, get rid of the unwanted audio information on either side of your chosen

eight-bar groove. Then, still with the Scissors tool, cut the file in half, leaving you with two four-bar sections of audio, one playing the first half of the rhythm and the other playing the second half.

3   Select the first piece of audio by clicking on it with the Pointer tool and double-click on the block, opening up the Audio Editor. Once you're inside the editor you'll see your cut piece of audio, spanning half the length of your initial section of audio – in this case, four bars.

4   Click on the end-inset point of the file, on the bottom-left-hand corner of the waveform, and drag to the right. You'll see the file extending and the previously discarded information coming into view again.

5   Apply the same process to the other half of the groove. This time, though, when you go into the Audio Editor, grab the start-inset point and pull it to the left to reveal the first four bars of the audio file.

Once you've altered the length of the file in the Audio Editor, this change will be reflected on the main Arrange page – in Cubase, your information block will expand to fill the required new space. If you see single arrows on the top left and bottom right of your audio file, you'll know that the file is fully extended. If you see double arrows at the start- and end-inset points, this means that the file has been altered and is only referencing part of its original length.

To enable you to snap your wave file to a bar position, you also have a Q flag, which is moved to the front of the audio file and enables you to line up the beginning of your wave with the beginning of a bar or line of any quantise subdivision you like.

The file itself can be dragged either way to be made shorter or it can be returned to its original length. All you're changing when you cut a piece of audio is the particular segment you're choosing to reference, because the Audio Editor is mainly a non-destructive editor – the representation of the file on your computer's hard drive hasn't changed. Finite editing of waveforms can be achieved relatively easily by using the start- and end-inset points and the magnifiers.

Tutorial 15: Selecting Audio Segments

Whether you're creating an exact four-bar drum sequence or choosing single drum hits from an audio recording, the selection process is the same, initially, as follows:

basic Rhythm Programming

1 Once you've roughly cut your piece of audio in the main Arrange page, select it and move into the Audio Editor by double-clicking on it.

2 Play the segment of audio and determine the start point (refer to the counting procedure in Chapter 2 if you have any problems). If you're making a loop, the beat should normally start on a bass-drum hit.

3 Move the start-inset point to the beginning of your loop by clicking and dragging. Be sure to turn off the MIDI and audio click in the main Arrange page during this process. At this point, the audio information will bear no relation to the speed of your sequencer, and an out-of-time click will be extremely confusing.

4 Click and drag the end-inset point to the end of your loop. If you've cut your rhythm too short, remember that the start- and end-inset points can be moved either to the left or to the right. For now, though, assume that the segment is slightly too big and has to be edited down to size.

5 Return to the start point of the loop and use the magnifiers to expand the waveform. You'll notice your bar scale changing as you decrease the

magnification, but don't worry – it will return to normal later. Increasing the magnification will allow you to move your start-inset point to the exact beginning of the loop.

6   Go to the end-inset point of your loop and repeat the process.

7   Play the loop and check that it's the exact length that you require. Make sure you haven't left it too short at the end.

8   Decrease the magnification to your normal scale.

9   Take the Q flag situated on the waveform and move it to the front of the loop, which will allow you to line up your loop exactly at the start of the bar.

For single drum hits, the procedure is exactly the same. Once you've moved your start- and end-inset points to the required positions, you can then move the selected drum voice around the editor, lining up with whatever beat you wish.

Tutorial 16: Creating A Groove

We'll start this procedure with a bass-and-snare groove, following on from the previous tutorial.

basic Rhythm Programming

1   Once you've roughly cut your piece of audio in the main Arrange page, have a look at it in the Audio Editor. If you're locating a single hit in the Arrange page, use the magnification sliders (located in the bottom-right-hand corner) to enable you to achieve an accurate cut. You might also need to turn off the Snap function because your bass-drum hit will probably bear no relevance to your click or bar-position indicator at this point.

2   Play the segment of audio and determine the start point.

3   Move the start-inset point to the beginning of the bass-drum beat by clicking and dragging. Then move the end-inset point to the end of the loop.

4   Return to the start of the loop and use the magnifiers to expand the waveform. Refine the position of your start-inset point under magnification so that it's exactly at the beginning of the bass-drum beat.

5   Go to the end point of the bass-drum sample and repeat the same process.

6   Play the segment and check that it's exactly the required length.

7   Decrease the magnification and return to normal scale.

8   Click on the Q flag (situated on the waveform) and move it to the front of the section. This will allow you to line up your chosen loop exactly with the start of a bar.

9   Create a copy of this bass-drum hit on the third beat of the bar by clicking on it, keeping your finger on the Alt key, and dragging it to the third beat in the bar, making sure your snap value is set to 4. You'll now have two bass-drum beats, one on beat 1 and one on beat 3.

10 Make another copy of your bass drum and move it downwards into another lane.

11 Next, expand out the waveform using the start- and end-inset points and locate a single snare-drum hit.

12 Isolate the snare hit by repeating the same process that you used for the bass.

13 Move the Q flag to the beginning of the snare hit and line it up with beat 2.

basic Rhythm Programming

14 Click on the snare-drum hit and, using the Alt key, make a copy and drag it to beat 4 in the bar. If you press Play on your sequencer now, you'll now have four single hits, giving you a basic drum groove.

15 Return to the main Arrange page, where you'll see a block of information that's bigger than your one-bar edited bass-drum and snare part.

16 Use the magnifiers to determine exactly where your bass-drum and snare hits lie. If you move the first bass-drum hit to the beginning of a bar in your Audio Editor, this position will be reflected in the Arrange page and you'll be able to cut your block of information easily by changing the snap setting to Snap To Bar.

17 Cut on both sides of the bar to get rid of your unwanted information blocks.

18 Select 'Repeat Parts' in the Structure menu and type in how many copies you require.

19 Select 'Do It' and your one-bar bass-drum-and-snare groove will be copied and will appear in the main Arrange page and the Audio Editor as separate blocks of information.

Of course, if you're working with single samples imported from a compiled CD-ROM, you probably won't have to edit the lengths of the samples. Nonetheless, this procedure is still relevant as, by copying and placing hits in the Audio Editor, you can create any groove you like and it can be as long as you wish.

It's important to remember that the placement of notes is determined by your snap value, so you should change that according to your own requirements for the track.

Tutorial 17: Quantising Loops And Changing Speeds

1   Create a loop in Cubase's Audio Editor.

2   Play your chosen segment of audio and determine the start point.

3   Move the start-inset point to the beginning of your loop and the end-inset point to the end. Again, increase the magnification and fine-tune these positions. Play the loop and make sure it's exactly the length you require, then return to normal scale.

4   Take the Q flag (which is situated on the waveform), move it to the front of your loop and line it up exactly to the start of a bar, as in the previous tutorial.

basic Rhythm Programming

5   Select your audio segment, go to the Do menu and
    select 'Get M Points'. If the audio part has had no
    match points calculated already, the Get Match
    Points dialog box will appear.

6   Click on the Process button to allow your sequencer
    to compute the match points for the selected part.

7   Still keeping the audio part selected, go to the Do
    menu again and this time choose 'Snip At M Points'.
    The groove will be split automatically into individual
    parts according to the settings chosen in the Get
    Match Points dialog box.

8   When the process is complete, you can use the
    Note-On Quantise function to adjust the feel or
    tempo of your recorded audio. For example, if you
    wanted to make your loop swing more, you could
    adjust the quantise setting in the Audio Editor to
    16T and press Q on the computer keyboard.

The action of chopping your loop into its composite
parts also allows you to adjust its tempo, although
there are limits to how far you can go with this – the
slower you go, the more gaps there are between the
audio hits, which can cause your audio loop to stutter.
Also, as you increase the tempo, the loop will start to

trip over itself. A shift in tempo of about 10–15bpm either way is usually the maximum.

Tutorial 18: Matching Tempo To Audio

This is an extremely useful function which allows you to match the tempo of your sequencer to the tempo of your loop. When this is achieved, you can start to build an arrangement incorporating your MIDI devices.

1   Once you've cut your piece of audio roughly in Cubase's main Arrange page, select it as before and open up the Audio Editor.

2   Play the segment of audio and determine the start point of your loop and fix your start- and end-inset points in place at the start and end of your loop, magnifying and fine-tuning to make sure things are really accurate.

3   Move the Q flag to the front of your loop as before, by clicking on it and dragging it to your required position with the Pointer tool.

4   Create a loop within the Audio Editor by moving your right and left locators to the desired positions (by double-clicking on the position boxes) and

activating the Loop function, situated just to the right of the top centre of the Audio Editor's window.

5   Set your sequencer's loop points to the same amount of bars as that of your audio loop.

You'll notice at this point that the loop length is indicated by a white bar running across the top of the page, and this will differ from the size of the audio file, even though they're both set to the same amount of bars. Our job is to match them up. Remember, though, that if your sequencer is running faster than your drum loop, the sequencer will finish a one-bar cycle faster than the time it takes for your one bar of audio material to complete its own one-bar cycle.

6   Once your wave file is at the start of a bar and the Loop function is turned on, select the file.

7   Go to the Do menu and select 'Fit Event To Loop Range'. A dialog box will appear asking if you would like to match the audio file to the tempo of your sequencer or match the sequencer to the tempo on the audio file. Choose 'Tempo'.

Once you've completed this procedure, your sequencer will match the tempo of your audio file perfectly, or at least it should do; it will all depend on whether you got the loop start and end points correct to start off with.

Tutorial 19: Matching Audio To Tempo

This process is the reverse of the previous tutorial and is used when you have elements of an arrangement that are working at a particular tempo and you wish to time-stretch or compress your audio loop to fit in with the tempo of your arrangement.

1   Import your chosen piece of audio into the Cubase Arrange page either by using the Import Audio function in the File menu or by importing directly into the Audio Pool and then dragging and dropping your audio directly onto the Arrange page.

2   Double-click on the audio part in the main Arrange page to open up the Audio Editor.

3   Move the start- and end-inset points to the beginning and end of your loop respectively, magnifying and fine-tuning as before.

4   Move the Q flag to the front of your loop as you did before.

basic Rhythm Programming

5 Again, create a loop within the Audio Editor by setting your right and left locators (by double-clicking on the position boxes) and activating the Loop function.

6 Set your sequencer's loop points to the same number of bars as your audio loop.

7 Once your wave file is at the start of a bar and the Loop function is turned on, select the file.

At this point, it's worth mentioning again that, once you've stretched your audio, you have only one level of undo, so unless you want to alter your audio file permanently, follow the procedure below:

8 Double-click on the file to open the Wave Editor and select the segment you're working on by pressing Ctrl (Apple Command) + A.

9 Go to the File menu and select 'Selection To File'. A File dialog box will appear. Rename your file and save it.

10 Return to the Audio Editor by pressing the Return key on the computer keyboard and delete the original file. You're now going to replace it with a

specially named backup. (A good name might be the original file name plus the new intended bpm – for example, 'Ex Break Hip-Hop 83bpm'.)

11 Go to the Audio Pool and drag and drop the new file into the Audio Editor. Make sure that it's in the same position as the previous file. Now you can do what you like with it. This procedure will enable you to back up any file during any audio operation.

12 Go to the Do menu and select 'Fit Event To Loop Range'. A Dialog box will appear asking if you'd like to match the audio file to the tempo of your sequencer or match the sequencer to the tempo on the audio file. Choose 'Audio'.

When the procedure is complete, your audio file will match perfectly the speed of your sequencer.

5 WORKING WITH MIDI AND AUDIO

Once you've recorded or imported your audio information into your sequencer, it will sit as blocks of information on your main Arrange page. Normally, these blocks will all be assigned to different channels on this page. Each channel is then routed to the virtual mixer, which will reflect the channel settings on the main Arrange page. The level of the audio is controlled by the mixer's faders. At this stage, you can also begin to assign plug-in effects, EQ, limiting, compression or gating to your audio.

The signal can now be routed to groups, which makes it easier to submix tracks that are in the same kind of category – for example, all of your drums may be assigned to one group, your keyboards may be grouped to another, and so on. This process will help you to balance all like tracks relative to each other.

After this stage, the signal travels to the master mixer, or, if you have a card that has more than two outputs, you can assign individual channels to their own bus outs. For example, if you had a card that had two record inputs and eight outputs, it would be possible to assign eight audio tracks to eight individual outputs, which would obviously give you a great deal of flexibility. The signal is sent from the card to your external mixer's inputs.

The Cubase Mixer

To access the main Cubase mixer, you can press Ctrl + (keypad) * (Apple Command + * on Mac) or go to the Panels menu and select 'VST Channel Mixer 1'. The mixer replicates the format of a traditional external mixer, with the output of each of your recorded channels represented by its own fader. You can alter the equalisation and assign effects to each channel on an individual basis.

The way in which you mix and balance your recorded information can alter radically the sound and feel of what you've played. However, it's worth bearing in mind the fact that, if your source sounds are recorded poorly, you won't be able to achieve a good drum mix.

On the Cubase monitor mixer, all of the channel strips contain the same parameters, except each applies to a separate audio channel on the Arrange page.

By breaking down and defining one strip, you should be able to navigate your way around the whole desk.

Cubase mixer channel settings

Input Select

This indicates the input that you're using. Stereo tracks
will have left and right inputs across two linked channel
strips – ie a stereo pair. Press Ctrl (or Apple Command
for Macs) and click on the input in order to toggle it
to left or right.

Insert

Pressing this button will allow you to apply insert effects
across your channel.

FX/EQ
Pressing this button will open your effects and EQ windows.

Mute
This will allow you to exclude a particular channel strip from the mix.

Solo
This is pretty much the opposite of the Mute function. Pressing this button will exclude all of your other tracks from the mix. This parameter is particularly useful if you want to concentrate on an individual drum part.

Pan
Stereo channels can be panned hard left and right to achieve a full stereo effect. Panning is a crucial part of the mixing process.

Clip Indicator
A red light will appear here if you're pushing too much level into a channel.

Input Level Indicator
Activating this will show you the amount of level going into Cubase during recording. Be warned, though – you can't alter the input level from the channel fader.

Level Meter
This monitors the level of output from Cubase.

Channel Fader
You can adjust the output volume of the signal on each channel by using the faders, allowing you to balance your various recorded instruments.

Fader Level Indicator
This is a numerical indicator depicting the volume of each channel.

Output Channel Name
The name of each channel will coincide with its corresponding channel name listed on the main Arrange page.

The main thing to remember is that, once you've become familiar with one channel, you know them all.

Converting MIDI To Audio
One of the most useful techniques employed by programmers is the conversion of recorded MIDI information into digital audio. At their most basic, MIDI recordings consist of Note On and Note Off trigger messages. Once you've recorded your MIDI information, it will be viewed as a separate audio file that you'll be

able to view on the virtual mixer, enabling you to use the vast array of plug-in effects, equalisation, compression and limiting capabilities associated with modern software sequencing packages.

When it comes to monitoring your triggered external sound modules, the usual technique is to take right and left stereo outputs from each module and plug them into two inputs of your external mixer. Internal soft synths and VST instruments, meanwhile, are monitored by taking a line out from the back of your soundcard and running it into a pair of your external mixer's line inputs.

VST instruments and audio instruments are already built in and routed through to Cubase's main mixer outputs, but external MIDI instruments are triggered only by your sequencer. In order to record these sounds into your software sequencer, you'll need to run an output from your external mixer into the input side of your soundcard. The signal then travels from the triggered sound module into the input of the external mixer. By assigning the sound module's input channels to two bus outputs (left and right), the sound is re-routed back through the external mixing desk and into the soundcard's inputs, via the VST Inputs, and then into Cubase.

Tutorial 20: Recording External Sound Modules

Once the basic routing is sorted out, the recording process is the same as for any normal recording. Take a look at the following procedure and have a go yourself.

1   In the main Cubase Arrange page, select an audio track by highlighting it with the mouse and selecting the appropriate track class in the Track Class column marked 'C', situated to the left of the main Arrange page.

2   Open the Inspector by clicking on the arrow icon, situated in the bottom-left-hand corner of the main Arrange page. Select 'Mono' or 'Stereo', as appropriate, and then 'Record Enable'.

3   Select which of the triggered sound sources you wish to record first. If you're triggering a number of MIDI sounds from the same module, you'll have to mute the sounds you don't wish to record. This is because, on most modules, there is only a stereo out, which means that all of their sounds are mixed internally within the modules themselves. The more outputs a module has, the more you can individualise different sounds onto different channels on an external mixer.

The most effective way of achieving separation is by recording each MIDI track one by one by using the Mute functions that are available in the main Arrange page or in the Drum Editor page. This will individualise the track you want to record and silence the MIDI tracks you don't wish to be included in that particular audio pass. (The Mute button is situated in the 'M' column on the main Arrange page and is next to every drum voice in Drum Editor.) This process will give you far greater flexibility in your final mix.

You can also choose which sounds you want to record from your external mixer by routing the required channels in your computer to your mixer's bus outs. This basically means that you don't have to record everything that's plugged into your external mixer – you can choose which sounds or modules are routed to the inputs of your soundcard.

4   To monitor your recording, open the main channel mixer and illuminate the 'In' button on your chosen channel strip. This will enable you to monitor the sound or collection of sounds being output from your external mixer into Cubase. Be aware that you can't change your input level from the internal mixer – this will have to be done from your external module, the

external mixer's output or your computer's Multimedia Setup dialog box via the Sound control panel (pre-OS X Macs) or the Panels menu (PCs).

5   Check your record levels.

6   Choose whether you want to make the recording in mono or stereo. (Most drum sounds will usually be recorded in mono.)

7   Choose an appropriate folder for your recorded audio.

8   Set your left and right locator positions to include the section that you wish to record.

9   Illuminate the Punch In and Punch Out icons on the main Transport bar, then rewind the sequencer and press Record. When the sequencer's position indicator hits the left locator, it will start to record, and when it hits the right locator, it will stop recording.

10 Check your recording.

11 Mute the MIDI part you've just recorded. Proceed to the next part and repeat the process.

The Wave Editor

The Wave Editor is where more detailed editing can be performed. The thing to remember is that all of the editing functions that take place in this editor are destructive (ie permanent) and are subject to only one level of undo, so it's advisable to make back-up copies of all of the audio files you're going to edit.

The Wave Editor has its own Play and Cycle buttons, which are situated at the top of the window. It also has its own Start and End Position buttons that enable you to move between exact start and end positions of your audio.

The thumbnail-view window that runs along the bottom of the Wave Editor window is used for reference purposes when performing more detailed editing. As the magnification of a waveform is increased, although you're able to edit your data more accurately, it becomes increasingly difficult to know exactly where you are in relation to the whole file, so this window is used as a guide to your overall position.

The Wave Editor Toolbox

The Wave Editor toolbox is accessed in the same way as the tools in the other editors. PC users will use a right mouse click.

Here's a brief run-down of the tools and their functions. Most of them are similar to the tools used in other editors and the main Arrange page, although their functions in the Wave Editor may be slightly different.

Pointer

This tool is used to highlight your waveform in order to edit it, and this may be done in two ways. To select the whole wave, hold down Ctrl (Apple Command) + A – this will enable you to select the whole segment represented in the main Arrange page and the Audio Editor. If you wish to change or edit a selected segment of your audio file, this can be done by clicking on the Pointer tool and dragging it across your audio segment. When a piece of audio is selected, it's shaded black.

Scrub

This tool replicates the effect caused by analogue tape moving across the record heads of a multitrack recorder. In order to locate the beginning of a bass-drum or snare-drum hit, you can click on the Scrub tool and drag it across your waveform.

Speaker

The Speaker tool will allow you to listen to your waveform from a selected point. To use the Speaker tool, move the icon to the audio segment you wish to reference, then click and hold down the mouse to play the particular part of the waveform that you want to hear.

Hand

This tool will enable you to move a selected audio segment left or right to a new position within the Audio Editor without changing the length of the file that's being played.

The Do Menu

Wave editors not only allow you to delete and edit unwanted material; they also enable you to change the shape and sound of what you've recorded. Using Cubase as an example, you can do this by using the functions in the Do menu, situated at the top-left-hand corner of the Wave Editor. I've listed the most widely used functions present in all audio editors below.

Reverse

Highlight the section of the file that you wish to edit and choose 'Reverse' from the Do menu to reverse your highlighted audio completely. This function can be very useful for creating interesting rhythmic patterns.

Fade In/Out

This will produce an automatic fade across your highlighted audio. You can also use this function at a

very high magnification to mask partially any unwanted
audio material.

Normalise

This function allows you to increase the overall level
of your audio file. When you choose 'Normalise', another
dialog box will appear enabling you to choose the level
by which you wish your file to be increased.

Quieten

This will give you a 6dB cut in your audio file, basically
cutting the volume of your recording by half. This can
be very useful if you want to eradicate background
noise in a recording.

Pitch Shift

I've already covered the process of matching audio to
tempo using the Audio Editor. In short, you can increase
or decrease the tempo of your audio with no deleterious
effect on the pitch of the original material. Also, the
pitch of a groove can be altered via the Pitch Shift
feature, which raises or lowers the pitch of a selected
segment of an audio file in semitones and cents. Many
drum-and-bass grooves use this feature.

To change the pitch of your material, highlight a section
using the Pointer tool and select 'Pitch Shift' from the

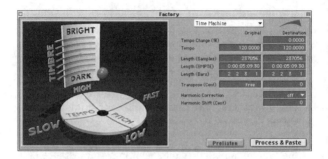

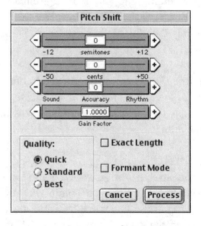

Logic Audio's Time And Pitch Machine (top) and Pitch Shift dialog box (bottom)

Do menu. Double-click on the 'Semitones' and 'Cents' boxes and enter in the required value for each. Activating the Formant mode will make the pitch shift sound natural, while the 'Exact Length' option allows the processed audio to remain the same length as the original. The 'Gain' factor enables you to lower the volume of your processed audio (sometimes pitch shifting will increase the level of the target audio file), whereas the 'Accuracy' option allows Cubase to prioritise the type of material it's pitch shifting – for instance, if you're changing the pitch of a drum groove, it's important for the timing to be as accurate as possible, and in this case the accuracy slider would be set to a low value.

Finally, the Quality option allows you to determine the quality of the audio processing. Of course, the higher the quality, the longer the computer takes to perform the operation.

Time Stretch

The Time Stretch option allows you to increase or decrease the length of your audio without suffering from a drop or rise in pitch. When you select a section of audio in the Wave Editor and select 'Time Stretch' from the drop-down menu, a dialog box will appear, as shown here:

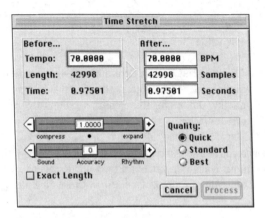

Cubase Time Stretch dialog box

- **Source File** – This is where you enter in the source tempo of your audio segment.

- **Destination File** – Enter the tempo that you wish the file to be stretched to.

- **Exact Length** – When this is selected, the length of the processed audio is exactly the same length as the original file.

- **Accuracy** – This enables you to prioritise between rhythmic and non-rhythmic processing. For rhythmic processing, set the accuracy slider to a low value.

- **Quality** – This setting determines the quality of the audio processing. Again, though, the higher the quality, the longer the computer takes to perform the operation.

Once you're aware of and have an understanding of the features available, you'll find that you're able to grasp the operation of any wave editor with relative ease.

6 STYLES

In this chapter, I'm going to be looking in depth at the programming traits associated with working in specific musical genres. Drawing on all of the skills you've learnt so far, I'm going to take you through interactive tutorials, which will highlight the changes in rhythmic patterns and sound associated with different styles.

Before we embark on this odyssey, though, it's worth mentioning the fact that, when you're programming, sound is everything. The sound of your drums can make a groove come alive, and it's often true that there's little mystery to a great groove. The most important thing to remember is that less is definitely more. Don't get too complicated in your approach. The temptation is to multilayer lots of MIDI and audio drum tracks, which is often extremely confusing to the listener. If you listen to the programmed drums in most genres, you'll find that simplicity is the key. Use the programming tools I've shown you in the previous chapters to create your own source sounds and to help you solve any programming situation you might encounter.

Industry-Standard Electronic Drum Sounds

Two drum kits that I have to mention here are the Roland TR808 and TR909 The preset drum sounds contained within these two electronic drum machines revolutionised the world of drum programming and the way in which most modern records are made. The drum sounds of the 808 are rather mellow, whereas the bass-drum and snare sounds sound particularly fat. Also, when the bass drum on the 808 is detuned, it turns into a low-end boom sound. The hi-hats, meanwhile, have a very top-end hissing sound. The 808 has been used on countless hip-hop tracks, and its sound is absolutely unmistakable.

The 909, on the other hand, has a far more punchy sound than that of the 808 and is often heard on more up-beat dance tracks. The 909 kick drum is one of the most widely used kick-drum samples ever and is present in many dance-orientated rhythms.

Importing MIDI And Audio Files

1   Open the main Arrange page of your sequencer.

2   Choose a MIDI track by highlighting a track in the Track column. Make sure your Track Class setting reflects the type of track you're importing (ie MIDI).

3   Select 'Import MIDI File' from the File menu.

4   A dialog box will appear. Navigate to an appropriate file and double-click on it.

5   Another dialog box will appear, this one asking if you'd like to merge the file into the current arrangement and if you'd like to include accents. If so, the new file will be merged into your arrangement at the left-locator position.

Now let's try importing audio files:

1   Follow the same procedure as that for importing MIDI files, but make sure that your Track Class setting is appropriate for an audio file and, instead of selecting 'Import MIDI File' from the File menu, choose 'Import Audio File'.

2   Navigate to a suitable file on your computer's hard drive or on a library CD-ROM.

3   Another dialog box will appear. At this point, you can audition your files. When you've found a file you wish to import, click Open.

You can also import several files at once into the Audio

Pool. (Logic Audio's Audio Pool is called the Audio window, although the importing procedure is pretty much the same.) To do this, follow the procedure detailed below:

1 Open the Audio Pool by selecting 'Audio Pool' from the Panels menu in the main Cubase toolbar.

2 In the Audio Pool window, select 'Import Audio' from the File menu. You can once again audition the audio files. Once you've chosen a file, press 'Open'. The chosen file will be imported directly into the Audio Pool.

3 Take the file directly into the Arrange window by dragging and dropping.

Audio files can also be imported directly into the Audio editor by taking the Pencil tool and clicking on a lane. A File dialog box is then opened in the normal way. The file will be merged into your arrangement and will position itself at the left-locator position.

Hip-Hop

Hip-hop is without doubt one of the biggest-selling music genres in the world. It basically evolved from DJs playing old-school funk records and realising that their audiences went mad during the drum and percussion breaks. Using two decks, they started repeating the percussion and drum breaks and mixing in vocals and music from other records, creating a new genre of music.

Hip-hop can be divided into four basic categories:

Breakbeat

Breakbeat is generally between 90bpm and 130bpm, and its grooves tend to be taken from old funk and Atlantic soul records. They are totally acoustic in nature, have a lo-fi sound and are normally contained within extremely hypnotic loops. The grooves are mainly hi-hat-driven and have a constant, unaccented sound. The main snare groove – which is normally placed on 2 and 4 – is supplemented by additional broken-16th-note snare beats or ghost notes that weave in and out of the main groove.

Snare Sounds

Breakbeat snare sounds tend to be comprised of real audio samples. They can be full-bodied or thin and acoustic in nature.

Bass-Drum Sounds

The bass-drum sounds associated with breakbeat are

also live-sounding in nature. An acoustic sample is often used to produce a live-sounding dull thud, which is then layered with a small electronic sample that moves air and provides clean bottom end.

Hi-Hat Sounds
Hi-hat sounds are, again, acoustic in nature and can be generated from single wave samples, or they can be electronic sounds layered over a loop-based acoustic rhythm.

Tom Sounds
Depending on the type of rhythm you're playing, you might not even use toms. However, the thing to remember is that fills are nearly always a part of the rhythm itself. Most breakbeat grooves don't resolve in the same way that a rock groove would – rather than bringing the groove to a grinding halt, tom fills accentuate and highlight the groove or become a recurring part of a repetitive loop.

Cymbal And Crash Sounds
In breakbeat, space is the important factor when using cymbal sounds. Your arrangement will normally dictate what type of cymbals you use or if you need any at all. Cymbals can be used to highlight a particular phrase or to mark the beginnings and end of sections. Also,

cymbal samples can be detuned to provide a range of effects, a process that can be done in the Wave Editor (for audio samples) or in the Transpose section of the MIDI Editor (for MIDI-driven samples).

Percussion Sounds

Percussion sounds can range from cow bells and handclaps to practically any sound you wish. In breakbeat, conga drums and tablas are sometimes used to provide atmosphere and set up a groove, while heavily detuned cymbals can sometimes be made to sound like gongs, which can give a slow breakbeat arrangement a sinister edge.

Electro

Electro grooves are almost always totally electronic in sound and can range from a light ambient feel to heavy, fat bass drums and snares, falling between 110 and 130bpm. The rhythms are extremely tight and machine-like and tend to demand a consistent thin 16th-note hi-hat sound, which can be achieved by making sure that the hi-hat sample you're using is light and your velocities are consistent. Also, there are normally tight 16th-note kick-drum hits that require a tight kick sample, which sometimes can be supplemented with a low-end boom kick drum that washes over the bottom end of the mix.

basic Rhythm Programming

Snare Sounds
Snare sounds are almost always electronic in nature and vary from big-sounding electronic hits to sharp, high-pitched, punched-crisp-packet-sounding noises.

Bass-Drum Sounds
Electro bass-drum sounds can be heavy, fat and overbearing or boom-like and ambient. The TR808 is a commonly used drum machine.

Hi-Hat Sounds
Tinny, thin hi-hats from the 808 series are used often in this genre.

Tom Sounds
The tom sounds found on the 808 are commonly used in electro as they are extremely electronic in nature and have a tiny sound, which means that they don't interfere with the flow and feel of the rhythm and instead become a part of the overall groove.

Cymbal Sounds
Cymbals in this type of hip-hop tend to be thin and high-pitched. This can be achieved by tuning them up in pitch, using the Pitch Shift function in the Wave Editor of your sequencer, or by tuning up individual samples in an external sound module.

Percussion Sounds

Percussion sounds can again range from cow bells and handclaps to practically any sound you wish. Sometimes conga drums and electronic rimshot sounds can be used to provide atmosphere and to supplement the groove. The percussion sounds often mimic part of the hi-hat pattern to add a sense of urgency to the groove.

Swung Hip-Hop

This feel is based on a 24-note quantise pattern – or, in musical terms, a 16th-note triplet feel. The triplets basically widen the space between the beats, which creates the swing feel. These grooves tend to have a sparse, uncluttered feel, taken at 85–100bpm, and the drum sound is thick, heavily dampened and very bottom-heavy with thin snare and hi-hat sounds.

Snare Sounds

In swung hip-hop, the snare can range from a dull, detuned thud to a high-end crack.

Bass-Drum Sounds

In this genre, bass-drums sounds are heavy, with lots of bottom-end gain, and the 808's sounds are often used for this purpose. (Remember that converting MIDI tracks to audio means that your sounds can be routed back through your mixing desk, providing you with the opportunity to re-equalise your sounds using the EQ on your external mixing desk and add warmth and fatness to your sound. Also, when your MIDI sounds are within the audio domain, you can use various plug-in effects within your sequencer to enhance and mould sounds to your track.)

Hi-Hat Sounds
In swung hip-hop, the hi-hat sound can be a deep, thick, crusty low-end sample or a tight, high, thin sound, depending on the particular type of flow you're going for.

Tom Sounds
Tom sounds should be tight and punchy and can either be electronic or acoustic in nature, with sizes in the higher register.

Cymbal And Crash Sounds
Once again, these will depend on the arrangement of your tune or rhythm, but in this type of hip-hop they tend to be extremely sparse.

Percussion Sounds
Percussion sounds can again range from live conga sounds to ethnic sounds and are used to provide atmosphere.

Trip-Hop

Trip-hop (65–90bpm) has a detuned, ambient feel and was initially created by slowing down old funk grooves in tempo and pitch and looping them.

Snare Sounds

The snare sound in trip-hop is detuned. To achieve this effect, jam the stick into the skin, ending your snare hit with a slight buzz, which will give the note length.

Bass-Drum Sounds

The bass drum has a dull thud and is acoustic in nature. You can also layer the bass-drum sound so that two hits are triggered at the same time. This will combine the raw, crusty nature of an acoustic bass-drum sound with the high-frequency punch of electronic sounds.

Hi-Hat Sounds

Normally, live loops or individual acoustic sounds are used in trip-hop, but you can pick out individual sounds from loops by using EQ. The hi-hat sound is thick, detuned and driving.

Tom Sounds

Again, the tom sounds are normally an intrinsic part of the overall loop. To give your groove interest and flow, use two or three different loops from the same take.

Cymbal And Crash Sounds

The ride cymbal in trip-hop has a big, washy, very compressed sound, but make sure you choose a sample that has definition. You can use detuned MIDI samples or, as discussed earlier, you can pitch-shift a single audio cymbal file in the Wave Editor.

Drum And Bass

Like hip-hop, drum-and-bass rhythms (160–180bpm) evolved from old-school funk grooves, which were sampled from records, cut up, rearranged and sped up with samplers or computers with music software.

The rhythms used in drum and bass can be extremely complex. They tend to have a light jazzy feel mainly due to the fact that the machines that were used to increase the tempo of the source breakbeat samples also took them up in pitch, giving them a thin, jazz-like sound. The older drum-and-bass rhythms have a really broken sound and are full of unexpected twists and turns on the bass drum and snare, reminiscent of jazz comping structure. This is probably why many of the newer jazz artists are latching onto the drum-and-bass sound and using it as a backdrop to their improvisations.

Most drum-and-bass music is formed around a basic heartbeat, which serves as the pulse of the groove in much the same way as the clave represents the fundamental pulse of Latin rhythms. The notes on the bass drum, hi-hat and snare should be played at a constant dynamic level. The drum sounds associated with this genre are listed below:

Snare Sounds

These can range from acoustic samples to thin, bead-like, hard electronic rock hits. The snare sound is normally played with a consistent dynamic and is light and even.

In many traditional drum-and-bass rhythms, the snare sound tends to contain many ghost notes that are extremely hard to replicate using single programmed samples. If you want to recreate this effect, expert use of your Velocity Controller in the MIDI Editor is an absolute must. Accentuate the main beat of the groove with the bass-drum and main snare pattern and fill in the other 16th-note spaces in your grid with varying degrees of low-velocity snare hits using a mellow light snare sample. Don't make things too cluttered, though – drum-and-bass grooves move at high tempos, so be careful or you could end up with a mess on your hands.

Bass-Drum Sounds

These can be either punchy or more boom-like and again can be parts of existing breaks or single samples.

basic Rhythm Programming

Traditional drum-and-bass rhythms have either crusty, acoustic samples or rock-hard electronic kick drums.

Hi-Hat Sounds
In drum and bass, the hi-hat sound tends to be thin and consistent due to the speed, and overly big sounds can clutter the feel. The hi-hat is played with a thin driving sound, with the tip of the stick struck on the top of the hat.

Tom Sounds
In drum and bass, the tom sounds can be either electronic or acoustic, while the sizes are in the higher register. Their sound tends to be thin, small and uncluttered.

Cymbal And Crash Sounds
Drum-and-bass ride cymbals tend to be very live-sounding and with a good deal of definition, particularly for that old-school breakbeat feel. Also, many of the rhythms have a ride cymbal or top part running in the background of the rhythm, providing a consistent flow and momentum. Using the bell of the ride, you can produce accent patterns to create rhythmic interest in the pattern. This technique is used often in drum and bass to break up the layered feel of some of the more intense, straighter patterns.

Hard Step

In sharp contrast to the broken, light feel of the previous rhythms, hard step is far more pounding and heavy-sounding.

Snare Sounds

In hard-step music, the snare has a straight feel, like a backbeat, with few skip notes and a rock-hard driving sound.

Bass-Drum Sounds

The bass drum has a thick, round sound, which can be achieved by using the 909's bass-drum sounds.

Hi-Hat Sounds

The hi-hat has a thin, light sound that keeps the flow and momentum of the groove. Running, consistent 16th-note patterns are sometimes used to give the groove an intense forward motion.

Modern R&B

Modern R&B (70–135bpm) is one of the most rhythmically challenging styles in current circulation. R&B places great emphasis on melody and tends to have a rather light feel. Almost all of the modern R&B you will hear will have programmed drums playing rhythms that contain combinations of live loops and

basic Rhythm Programming

MIDI-triggered sounds. Many of the most prominent breakthroughs in modern R&B have been made by DJs and producers who have come up with some incredible programmed grooves that act as a backdrop for the more traditional rap and vocal melody lines. The groove is repetitive and the instrumentation and vocals weave around a central rhythmic structure.

Modern R&B drum grooves sound amazing when reproduced on a totally acoustic loop. You can layer electronic bass-drum, hi-hat and snare sounds with a live loop, using the Match Quantise function mentioned earlier – this will rhythmically combine your audio and MIDI information. Electronic sounds are used to add more weight and colour to the groove and the live loop provides the human feel. The grooves are extremely diverse and can vary from heavily swung triplet feels to overly straight one-handed eighth- and 16-note feels that chop and change according to the melody line of the tune. The overall feel of the music is tight and accurate, so don't over-use accents and be sure to keep your hi-hat, snare and bass-drum parts dynamically consistent. Modern R&B also has a distinct lack of toms and traditional drum fills, and so, rather than putting more notes in to create tension, try dropping bass-drum and snare hits out of the overall mix to create holes.

New Jack Swing

New jack swing is based around a traditional modern R&B feel. These grooves are extremely repetitive and tend to have a traditional looped quality about them. The hi-hats have a consistent rolling feel and may have a shaker pattern weaving around them. The rhythm is programmed using a 16T quantise setting (ie six 16th notes to one crotchet).

Straight Time Feels

Not all modern R&B rhythms are programmed using a triplet feel; some are extremely straight in nature, and the bass-drum and snare patterns in these grooves are usually littered with rhythmic displacements, either random or in four- or eight-bar loops. Also, the hi-hat patterns are usually combined with broken 16th- or 32nd-note percussion patterns running alongside, providing a sense of urgency. Often, the drums follow exactly the programmed bass or keyboard parts providing the main melody, and this is achieved by copying the bass line or melody line and moving the new part to a drum track. Double-click on the new part to reassign the drum trigger hits to the relevant note numbers.

Snare Sounds

Modern R&B snare drums tend to be dry and sharp-sounding, with a top-end crack. The sounds can range

basic Rhythm Programming

from a table-top sound to a warm, full-bodied, thin sound. On the live side, 13in by 7in snares provide a thin, full-bodied sound.

Bass-Drum Sounds
In modern R&B, bottom-heavy bass drums are often used (normally from the TR808 family), as well as thin hi-hats. You'll also find shakers and percussive noises weaving in and around the basic groove, adding colour.

Hi-Hat Sounds
The hi-hats again tend to be thin and electronic in nature, generated typically by such devices as the TR808, or they can be extremely live and natural in feel.

Tom Sounds
Like I said, toms may not even be used in R&B grooves. As with hip-hop, fills are nearly always part of the rhythm itself, so tom fills don't bring the groove to a grinding halt, unless used in a dramatic ballad. Instead, they should accentuate the groove.

Cymbal And Crash Sounds
As with dance music, in modern R&B, tight, short sounds are used to keep the momentum and flow of the track. Also, you can alter the pitch of the cymbals to highlight sections or percussive phrases.

Percussion Sounds

Again, percussion sounds can be sourced from cow bells, handclaps or practically any sound you wish to produce. Sometimes conga drums and tablas can be used to provide atmosphere and set up a groove, while shakers can give a rasping, rhythmic edge to the sound.

Garage

Garage music is over 20 years old, and its roots stem from disco, which waned in popularity in the late '70s early '80s. It has a distinctive sound, which was created by disco producers and DJs continuing to make records for a minority market. As the record companies pulled their funding, there was no money to employ 40-piece orchestras and expensive session musicians, so the musicians who worked in the genre used cheap keyboards and drum machines to reproduce the sounds they wanted. Garage rhythms are computer-driven and tend to be very driving and up-front.

As garage music has progressed, its tempo and grooves have changed. Early garage grooves were fairly simplistic, with the bass drum falling on every crotchet and open hi-hats marking the upbeats, with the snare on beats 2 and 4. As the genre progressed, the grooves sped up and the amount of subdivisions on the bass drum and snare increased, and percussion and effects were added to the rhythm tracks.

There are four main sub-genres of garage, as follows.

Traditional Garage

Traditional garage grooves (120–130bpm) have the bass drum marking the quarter-note pulse and the snare playing on the second and fourth quarter notes in the bar. Skip snares and bass drums are added to create rhythmic interest and to help the groove flow. The main snare is sometimes replaced or layered with an electronic handclap, and instead of a traditional drum fill, various sections of the arrangement are marked with bass-drum and cymbal hits played simultaneously. If you're recording or playing in a traditional garage style, making your initial velocities consistent will make the rhythm drive.

Speed Garage

Speed garage heralded the return to prominence of the garage scene in 1997, marked by an increase in tempo of about 10–20bpm to around 140–160bpm. The grooves sounded less smooth, had a lighter, more intense feel and began to include hip-hop and funk breakbeats instead of the typical incessant, four-to-the-floor bass-drum pattern.

Two-Step

Two-step (140–160bpm) is more of a continuation of speed garage, but it also has a drum-and-bass influence in that the bass lines are deep and raw-sounding and tend to dominate the tracks in the same way that drum-and-bass lines do. The drums have a light feel and also borrow breakbeats from funk and hip-hop. Meanwhile, the hi-hat pattern has a disjointed shuffle feel. The grooves themselves sound clean and very machine-like.

The drum sounds associated with garage are as follows:

Snare Sounds

The snare drums used in garage tend to be dry and sharp-sounding, with a noticeable top-end crack, while the more traditional-sounding grooves tend to use the sound of a handclap either to augment or replace the main backbeat snare.

Bass-Drum Sounds

Bottom-heavy bass drums are often used, normally from the TR909 family of drum machines.

Hi-Hat Sounds

The hi-hats tend to be thin and electronic-sounding, such as those produced by the TR808 or TR909.

basic Rhythm Programming

Tom Sounds
Fills are not overly common in garage – the bass drum and snare are often used to build and punctuate sections.

Cymbal And Crash Sounds
Garage uses tight, short sounds to keep the momentum and flow of the track. Pitch-altering is again also common.

Percussion Sounds
Percussion sounds in garage can range from handclaps to shakers. Percussive noises also weave around the basic groove to add colour.

Rock
Rock-drum programming comes in many shapes and sizes – grooves can vary in tempo and intensity. Because the genre is so vast, the easiest way to explain the programming of rock music is through the techniques used in its arrangement. Basically, the programming of rock drums follows the structure of the song in question, and grooves resolve and are programmed in sections, such as verse, chorus, middle-eight, outro, etc.

In dance music, grooves maintain a constant theme and tension is created by elements of the main groove being added to or dropping out of the mix. In rock music, a groove will weave in and out of the main melody line and the voicing of the groove will change as the song progresses. An example of this might be moving from a hi-hat pattern in the verse of a song to a ride cymbal in a chorus to give the chorus an additional lift.

Rock grooves can be any tempo or time signature and they will draw from their immediate surroundings. One such example of this is rock bands incorporating hip-hop beats and loop structures into their arrangements. It's a genre of music that basically reflects the times, purely because it's based so much on songs and lyrics and not wholly influenced by DJs. All music genres will have an influence on rock, and vice versa. Traditionally, however, there are sounds and grooves that lend themselves to a rock feel.

Many of the newer rock styles have drawn influence from computerised rhythms and now use processed sounds to articulate a feel and an attitude. Due to the nature of the surrounding instrumentation, most traditional rock sounds tend to be acoustic in nature, either using loops or comprising single samples. Here are some of the more traditional sounds.

Snare Sounds

Rock snare drums can be deep and ambient or tight and thin-sounding to enable a snare to cut through a mix. An element of overtone is therefore important. This will also add to the live feel if you're programming using single hits.

Bass-Drum Sounds

Normally, rock bass drums are dampened so that they punch through a mix. The drums are fat and full-bodied, although in recent years they have become smaller-sounding with a lot of top-end slap being added to the sound to enable fast double bass-drum patterns to cut through without swamping a mix.

Note: Slightly detuning snares and bass drums can help to give a track body, but be careful not to conflict with the tuning of the other instruments.

Hi-Hat Sounds

Rock hi-hats range from an open, extremely trashy hi-hat to a tight, closed, crisp sound. It pays to choose your hi-hat samples carefully – if they sound too mechanical, they can really give the game away.

Tom Sounds

In rock, toms can range from tiny 6in models to a heavy 18in floor tom. If you're using the toms to articulate a whole groove or a fill, a range of tom sounds, from high to low, can be used to create rhythmic and sonic interest. If you're using the toms to drive a tune, you're best off going for the lower 14–18in toms, as these provide a driving low end to a groove.

Ride Cymbal And Crash Sounds

In rock music, crash cymbals can be used either to highlight accents within an arrangement or to punctuate the beginnings and ends of phrases or sections. Therefore, there's no particular standard sound or size of cymbal. The best thing you can do is audition various cymbal sounds and choose a selection that fits.

Ride cymbals tent to be cutting and heavy-sounding in rock, enabling them to be heard behind a wall of guitars. If you're programming a rock ride cymbal, you might want to toggle between playing on the bell of the cymbal, in order to produce accent patterns, and on the main body to create rhythmic interest.

Percussion Sounds

These can vary from ethnic sounds to road-drill samples, depending on how heavy-duty you want to get! Because the genre is so diverse and straddles most continents in the world, there are no real hard-and-fast rules governing what percussion sounds should be used in a particular track. Trust your ears and remember to reference similar music – don't copy, but do be inspired by others.

Funk

The drum rhythms used in funk are similar to those found in rock, in the fact that their influence has spread throughout every aspect of modern-day music. The subdivision traits and musicality of funk rhythms have been responsible for almost all of the contemporary forms of dance music that we know today. Due to the repetitive nature of funk grooves, they were used as the basis of the very first audio loops and were supplied as demo patterns with the first generation of samplers, thus giving birth to a new form of music-making.

Funk rhythms – typically taken at anything between 60 and 170bpm – are generally repetitive, establishing a theme that is then embellished upon using subtle voicings. The drums provide the main backbeat to the rhythm while all of the other instruments change around the central drum pattern. Many funk tracks are vocals- and arrangement-led, but unlike rock grooves, which think nothing of resolving and breaking up a rhythmic theme, funk patterns highlight changes while keeping the momentum of the groove.

Funk Drum Sounds
Snare Sounds

In funk, snare sounds can vary tremendously and can be either acoustic or electronic, depending on what you're looking for. Any of the above grooves that include 16th-note ghosting will need to be programmed using at least two different snares: a hard-hitting sound for the backbeat and a mellow, low-velocity sound for the ghost notes. Depending on the rhythm being played, the snare will either play a backbeat or interact with the ride cymbal, hi-hats and bass drum to create the overall rhythmic feel.

Bass-Drum Sounds
Old-school funk grooves tend to have heavily dampened bass-drum sounds imbuing a mix with warmth and punch. Bass-drum sounds can vary greatly from one funk groove to another, but they're generally one of the main rhythmic voices.

Hi-Hat Sounds
In funk, hi-hat sounds can be crisp and tight or mellow and dark, and open hi-hats are often used to accentuate certain passages. You'll normally want to match closely the two hi-hat samples you're using – the open hi-hat should blend with the closed hi-hat in tone.

Tom Sounds
The toms used in funk can range from a tiny 6in drum to a heavy 16in floor tom. In old-school funk, the rhythms played by the toms are mainly dampened. If

they're being used to articulate a fill, a range of tom sounds from high to low can be used to create rhythmic and sonic interest. The important thing to remember is that normally the fill is always a part of the rhythmic flow of the groove and doesn't break the groove. People's heads have to keep nodding!

Ride Cymbal And Crash Sounds

Funk crash cymbals aren't as heavy-sounding as rock crashes; they're thinner and higher in pitch, which keeps the momentum of the groove going. They can be used either to highlight accents within an arrangement or to punctuate the beginnings and ends of phrases or sections, so there's no particular standard sound or size of funk crash. The best thing you can do is audition various cymbal sounds and choose a selection that fits.

In funk, ride cymbals tent to be defined but mellow and lower in pitch than rock rides. This enables them to blend with the other instruments, such as pianos and guitars. Again, it's common to articulate some ride lines on the bell of the cymbal, and many funk grooves use the bell as an accent feature.

Percussion Sounds

Funk percussion can vary from ethnic sounds to Latin percussion sounds such as congas, bongos, cowbells and timbales. As with rock, because the genre is so diverse, there are no real rules.

Latin

The heartbeat of Latin music is the *clave*, a repeating 'two-three' or 'three-two' pattern. *Latin music* is sometimes a global term used to describe music from Brazil, such as samba, and also Afro-Cuban music.

Traditionally, Brazilian and Afro-Cuban rhythms were never played on modern drum sets; they were created using other forms of percussion instrument. Each instrument would play a particular part of the rhythm and their interactions would be the basis of each piece. However, Latin rhythms have been embraced by many new music genres, such as dance and drum and bass, which have adopted the polyrhythmic elements of the grooves and their percussive nature to add interest to their own drum arrangements.

Samba

Samba rhythms fall typically in the range of 60–200bpm and don't follow the main clave as strictly as Afro-Cuban rhythms do. The samba has a rolling bass-drum rhythm, traditionally played on the surdo drum, which gives a big, fat, low-end sound. The cymbal line drives the pattern along and interacts with the snare to provide rhythmic interest. The hi-hat is played with the foot on the second and fourth beat of every bar and acts as an anchor, along with the bass drum.

Afro-Cuban

Afro-Cuban grooves (70–150bpm) are much more broken in feel than samba rhythms and adhere very strictly to the clave. On a modern drum set, the ride cymbal takes the place of the cow-bell part, the toms replace the congas and a rimshot sound can be used as a conga slap. Normally, the most effective way of integrating an Afro-Cuban feel into a groove is to use a loop from a record that itself oozes feel and groove, although if you only want to take elements of the overall part to enhance your track, you'll have to use separate samples.

Latin Drum Sounds
Snare Sounds

The snare tends to be mellow and extremely velocity-sensitive, mostly operating in a reactive capacity. Depending on the rhythm being played, the snare will either play a backbeat or interact with the ride cymbal and other drums to add to the overall rhythmic feel.

Bass-Drum Sounds

Latin bass drums are often non-defined, quiet and ambient-sounding, which helps them to create a rolling feel without intruding too much. Sometimes the bass drum can be used to drive the track and provide a pounding, relentless, hard-edged rhythmic feel.

Hi-Hat Sounds

The hi-hat can provide either a rolling, accented feel that's low and muted in tone or it can simply be played on the second and fourth beats of the bar to provide a rhythmic anchor. In Afro-Cuban grooves, the clave is often played on the hi-hat.

Tom Sounds

Toms can be used to replicate conga lines if the rhythm has been transposed from separate percussion instruments to a drum set. In this case, a wide range of tom sounds are used to produce the desired rhythmic effect. In the case of Brazilian surdo grooves, large floor toms are used to give the groove depth.

Cymbal And Crash Sounds

The bell of a ride cymbal is often used to replicate a cow bell. Crash cymbals are used to highlight sections in the music and to punctuate phrases.

Percussion Sounds

The best way to absorb the feel and attitude of both Brazilian and Afro-Cuban rhythms is to listen to them on record. Some of the most common percussion sounds used are bongos, congas, timbale, cow bells and claves.

Dance

There are many different forms of dance music, all of which use the basic four-to-the-floor rhythm. One of the main traits of a dance rhythm is that most programmers will use the bass drum as their main starting point, normally programming four beats to the bar in a 4/4 time signature. Depending on the exact type of dance genre being programmed, the tempo will vary from between 130bpm to over 200bpm.

One overwhelming feature of dance music is its repetitive and hypnotic quality, and one of the main things that will help you achieve this is making sure that your bass-drum, hi-hat and snare velocities are consistent between beats. If the bass drum varies from one beat to another, it will detract greatly from the other instruments.

Once you've established your basic bass-drum pattern, the hi-hat plays against it on the upbeat, the two sounds comprising your basic dance heartbeat. The other instruments weave in and out of the main kick-drum-and-hi-hat pattern, creating a rhythmic counterpoint, as with funk grooves. Dance grooves tend to be wholly machine-based, but they do often have live percussion sounds added to enhance the overall feel and to provide rhythmic interest.

Techno

Techno (120–160bpm) originated in Detroit in the mid 1980s and uses electronic beats that are driving and intense. Techno rhythms run at extremely fast tempos and also use the four-to-the-floor bass-drum rhythm as their heartbeat. Over the past few years, techno has influenced many forms of music, from drum and bass to hardcore rock.

Tech Step

At 180bpm and above, tech step is a fusion between drum and bass and techno. The bass drum tends to land on the first beat of the bar and on the 'and' of the third beat (ie 'one-and-two-and-three-*and*-four-and'). Snare hits occur mostly on the second and fourth beats of the bar.

Ambient

This genre is based largely on atmospheric noise and as such is spacious and trance-like. With speeds falling typically somewhere between 60 and 100bpm, the rhythms associated with ambient music are mellow and hypnotic, and live-sounding loops are often used, employing sounds that are often ethnic and tribal in nature. When approaching the programming of ambient music, you should be thinking of creating a soundscape, as opposed to generating a driving rhythmic feel – although, having said that, over the past few years ambient has become more drum-orientated, spawning such offshoots as ambient dub, which merges hip-hop breakbeats over reggae bass lines with spacious synth delays, and ambient pop, which combines traditional rock and pop grooves with spacious sounds and vocals.

Trance

Trance is a psychedelic-sounding genre that combines elements of techno with psychedelia. It took many of its groove traits from dance music, particularly the four-to-the-floor kick drum and the relentless upbeat pattern of the hi-hat. The introduction of another Roland machine, the TB303, over a basic dance heartbeat – along with a blend of speaker-shifting effects, a driving 16th-note machine-generated bass line and effected percussion sounds – gave trance an unmistakable sound. The basic beat is relentless, with sudden drops, and builds in the programming structure. Keeping your individual drum parts on separate tracks will enable you to drop elements of your groove in and out of the overall mix to create rhythmic interest. Also, controller data such as filtering and LFO (Low-Frequency Oscillator) sweeps can be applied to separate parts of your drum arrangement. The drum sounds in trance music are almost wholly electronic in nature and once again often feature sounds from the Roland 909 family.

The drum sounds associated with the whole genre of dance are listed below. With dance tracks, you'll often find that live top-end loops are tucked underneath the main groove to provide a human element to the track, but this totally depends on the particular sub-genre. However, it's generally true that the harder-edged beats are generally stark, bare and intense-sounding, while looser tracks are more prone to adopting live loops and percussion sounds. (Remember, converting audio to MIDI template in Logic will enable you to match the feel of your audio and MIDI data.)

Snare Sounds

The classic dance drum sounds are produced by the Roland TR909 kit.

Bass-Drum Sounds

Depending on the particular genre of dance you're working within, the bass-drum sounds can be either small and punchy or overdriven and slightly distorted and can also have a plastic quality. Again, the TR909 produces the classic bass-drum sound.

Hi-Hat Sounds

Hi-hats are again from the 909 or 808 family and are either slightly distorted or have a top-end edge to them, which helps them to cut through a mix and gives them intensity.

Tom Sounds

Toms are either not used at all or they can feature in a track to produce a tribal feel.

Cymbal And Crash Sounds

Normally, tight, short sounds are used to keep the momentum and flow of a dance track, and you can achieve this effect by reducing the decay times of your samples. Also, you can alter the pitch of the cymbals to highlight sections or percussive phrases.

Percussion Sounds

In dance music, Latin sounds such as congas, bongos and timbales are often used to create a certain type of feel, an attitude. Some tracks will contain live Latin percussion sounds, but often the desired result is an intense, non-human intensity, so Latin machine drums are used. Also, African sounds and rhythmic feels are often super-imposed over the basic four-to-the-floor kick-drum pattern to contribute to the tribal feel. When it comes to ambient music, ethnic instrumentation is often used alongside live loops.

Remember that you can use the Quantise function to vary the feel of your recorded grooves, and that MIDI controllers can be used to filter elements of your groove in order to add sonic interest.

The Dance Dynamic Snare Roll

The dynamic snare roll is one of the main features that distinguishes dance drum programming from many other genres. The basic roll is led by the snare drum and gradually builds in velocity, intensity and frequency. The purpose of the roll is to announce a change in musical intensity. The snare roll can occur at any part of the arrangement and can end in a musical drop-down or bring the listener to a more intense part of the tune.

The basis of the snare roll is a consistent stream of 16th notes with no obvious accent programming. There is no set bar length, but the time signature will be 4/4. The roll will nearly always increase steadily in volume, gradually building to a crescendo at a pre-designated point in the arrangement. The roll will often be fuelled by a four-to-the-floor kick drum that will then join the snare as the intensity builds. Often, cymbals will also be added to the mix at key points to coincide with the addition of new instrumentation during the build. Multiple snares can also be used, each at a slightly different tuning to raise the pitch of the roll as it reaches its climax.

OK, fine. But how do we achieve this madness?

Tutorial 21: Roll Graduation

To achieve this effect, the initial quantise setting on the main Arrange page should be 16.

1   Select a new track to record on and mute all of your previously recorded material. Change the MIDI channel to 10.

2   Record a full bar of a snare pattern that falls on each quarter-note pulse.

3   We're going to make the snare roll eight bars long, so go to the Structure menu and select 'Repeat Parts'. This will add a series of repeats to your original one-bar riff, so choose a value of 7 in the dialog box, then click on 'Do It'.

4   You should now have blocks of information totalling

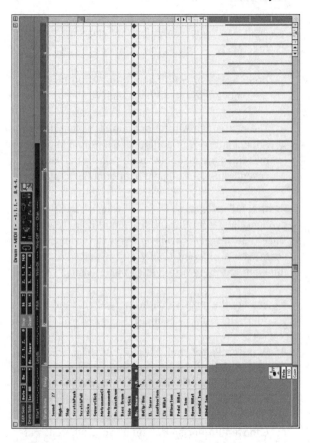

Cubase Key Editor showing snare hits and velocity information

eight bars. Select the Glue tool and stick them all together.

5   Double-click on your snare information block and then move into the editing window.

6   The next stage will be done in step time. In your Audio Editor, insert additional bass-drum and snare hits within the 16th-note pulses, leaving the key beats covering the four original quarter notes in place.

As the roll progresses, you'll want it to increase dynamically and in the subdivision of its note values. Once that has been achieved, you can layer another snare with a different tuning on the last two bars of the eight-bar pattern to add to the intensity.

7   Change the snap value in the grid to 32nd notes. Your grid will now change.

8   With the Pencil tool, fill in all of the blank snare note boxes in the last two bars of the eight-bar cycle. This will give a doubling effect to the last two bars. Make sure that your note placement is correct.

9   Choose another snare sound on a different note number. (If you want to work with the same sound

again, press Return and move back into the main Arrange page, move to a different MIDI channel and choose the same patch.) Instead of creating the part again, highlight the previously recorded block of information, hold down the Alt key on the computer keyboard and copy the recorded part onto a separate track with a different MIDI channel assignment.

We want to increase the pitch of this new part gradually as the roll progresses through its eight-bar cycle. To do this, mute the previous part to avoid confusion.

10 Return to the beginning of the roll and press Record. As the roll plays back, adjust the pitch-bend wheel on your controller keyboard gradually so that the pitch of your roll gets higher in pitch as the subdivision intensifies.

11 You have now added default pitch controller information to your existing data. To edit it, double-click on your recorded part and call up the Audio Editor. Bring up the controller icon situated in the bottom-left-hand corner of the window and bring up the Pitch Edit window, which will show your additional pitch-control information. This can be edited using the Pencil tool or erased using the Eraser tool.

basic Rhythm Programming

12 Return to the main Arrange page and listen to the two rolls together. If you want the pitched roll to occur at a certain place within your arrangement, you can do your further editing there by using the Scissors tool to cut out the section and stick it in the relevant place.

13 Now you'll need to add dynamics to your roll. First of all, mute out the pitched snare take.

14 Double-click on your original track and enter into the Audio Editor. The snare roll's volume will be shown in the Velocity Controller window, situated above the Velocity Controller icon on the bottom-left-hand side of the Cubase Drum or Key Edit window.

15 Select the Crosshairs tool from the toolbox, then go to the start of the first beat of the snare roll and click on the first velocity bar. While holding down the mouse button, drag the Crosshairs tool across the velocity window. As you do so, you'll be leaving a thin pencil line, drawing in your dynamic rise.

16 Once you've reached the end of the eight-bar phrase, let go of the mouse. You will now see that your velocity bars will have adjusted to the incline of your line, and your roll will be graduated. (Individual notes

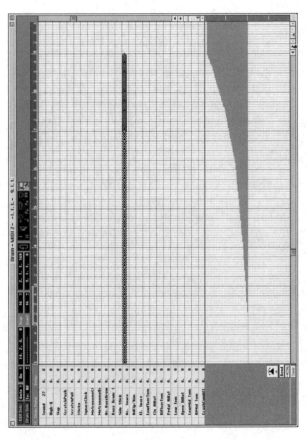

Pitched MIDI drum roll

can still be adjusted by using the Pencil tool.) Now you can repeat this technique for the pitched roll.

17 Cymbals and bass drums are normally added to mark sections in the roll, also increasing in subdivision as the roll reaches its climax. Their velocities and dynamics can be adjusted in the same manner as that described above.

As mentioned earlier, by using your controller editor, you can manipulate a number of controllers in this way. All of the controllers you use will work independently of each other. The Velocity Controller is the easiest controller to start with and is directly applicable to drums.

7 PROGRAMMING IN ODD TIMES

There are two parts to the programming of rhythms that aren't based on a regular, common-or-garden 4/4 time feel. The first task is to understand the concept of what odd times actually are and the second is to actually master the procedure of programming in these rhythms in your sequencing package. With this in mind, I'll take you through four tutorials designed to help you to get your head around the concept of odd time signatures.

First of all, though, let's talk a little about time signatures. Following on from the section on 'Note Values' in Chapter 2, you should be familiar by now with the concept of recording something in 4/4, by far the most common time signature in modern pop music. In conventional music notation, these numbers are stacked one above the other, with the upper figure determining how many beats there are to a bar (in this case, four) and the lower giving you the value of those beats (quarter notes). Similarly, 5/4 indicates that there are five quarter notes to each bar, while 6/8 indicates that there are six eighth notes to every bar. These notes can then be equally divided into any subdivision, depending on how fast or slow you want your resolution to be. For instance:

- A 5/4 bar divided into eighth notes will contain ten of them – ie ten equal beats passing in the time it takes to complete one bar.

- A 5/4 bar divided into 16th notes will contain 20 of them – ie 20 equal beats passing in the time it takes to complete one bar.

- A 6/8 bar divided into eighth notes will contain six of them – ie six equally spaced eighth notes will pass in the time it takes to complete one bar.

- A 7/8 bar divided into eighth notes will contain seven of them – ie seven equally spaced eighth notes will pass in the time it takes to complete one bar.

Remember that this same method applies to whatever time signature you're working in.

Recording Odd Time Signatures

At this point, you might find it useful to refer back to the 'Fast-Track Recording Guide' in Chapter 2. Bear in mind that, when you're getting used to working in odd times, it's extremely useful to count out loud! Here's how you record in 5/4:

1   Set the time signature on your sequencer to 5/4 by double-clicking on the Time Signature box on the Transport bar and entering the new time signature.

2   Press Play with the mouse. The sequencer's default click setting will be quarter notes. Listen to it and start to count out loud in groups of five – 'one, two, three, four, five'. And again – 'one, two, three, four, five'. Make sure that your vocalisation is in time with the click.

3   Continue this for a minute or two, then press Stop on the sequencer and return your position indicator to the start of beat 1.

As I've already indicated, once you've established your count, each of your five quarter-note pulses can be subdivided.

Tutorial 22: Recording An Eighth-Note 5/4 Groove

For this particular groove, we'll be using eighth notes for the hi-hat pattern.

1   Go to the Time Signature box in the Transport bar and change the time signature to 5/4.

2   Click on the hi-hat part in your Track List and move into an editor. Using either the Pencil tool or the Drumstick tool, depending on which editor you're working in, write in ten evenly spaced hi-hat pulses, two to each quarter note.

3   The bass drum and snare are going to remain on beats 2 and 4 and 1 and 3 respectively – this means that they can be punched in in the same way as the hi-hat.

4   Once this is done, return to the main Arrange page, set your locator positions to either side of the one-bar block and press Cycle on the Transport bar. You should now hear a rhythm in 5/4.

Tutorial 23: Recording A 12/8 pattern

1   Set the quantise value to 16T in the main Arrange page. This quantise setting will take back your sequencer's correction facility to 16th-note triplets, dividing each of your beats into four equal segments, each segment containing three eighth-note triplets.

2   In the main Arrange page, select a track and choose
    your hi-hat sample, then go to the Transport bar
    and change your time signature to 12/8.

3   Press Record. The hi-hat pattern you're about to
    record will cover all four segments of your four
    quarter-note triplet pulses, so your count-in will be
    'one-two-three, two-two-three, three-two-three, four-
    two-three'.

4   As soon as the two-bar click precount has elapsed,
    start recording. When you've completed your one-
    bar cycle, stop and listen back to your recording.

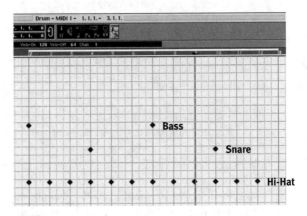

Cubase Drum Editor showing a 12/8 recorded rhythm

5 Double-click on your hi-hat information block and move into your editing window. Set the quantise value to 16T in the Quantise dialog box and press 'Q' on your computer keyboard. (Logic users can choose the Q function on the main Arrange page or in the Matrix Editor.)

6 Programming in step time, draw in bass-drum hits on beats 1 and 3 and snare hits on beats 2 and 4.

7 Once this is done, return to the main Arrange page and set your locator positions on either side of the one-bar block. Press Cycle on the main Transport bar. You should now hear a rhythm in 12/8.

Tutorial 24: Recording A 7/8 Pattern

1 First, set your quantise value to eighth notes on the main Arrange page.

2 In the Arrange page, select a track to record on, set it to record hi-hats on channel 10 and change the time-signature value in the Transport bar to 7/8.

3 Press Record. Once the count-in has passed ('one-two-three-four-five-six-seven'), record hi-hat hits on each beat. When you've got a full bar, press Stop.

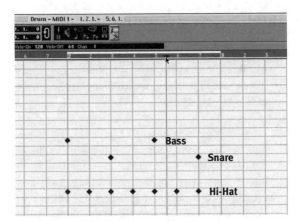

Cubase Drum Editor showing a 7/8 recorded rhythm

4 Double-click on the part and move into your editing window. Using either the Pencil or the Drumstick tool, depending on which editor you're working in, place seven evenly spaced hi-hat pulses covering each of the seven eighth-note segments. Punch in bass-drum hits on the first and fifth eighth notes and snare hits on the third and seventh.

5 Return to the main Arrange page and set your locator positions on either side of the one-bar block. Press Cycle on the main Transport bar and you should hear a rhythm in 7/8.

Tutorial 25: Recording A 5/8 Pattern

1 Set up your sequencer as in the previous tutorial, but this time set the time-signature value in the dialog box to '5/8' and record a one-bar sequence of five hi-hat pulses.

2 Programming in step time in your chosen editor, punch in bass-drum hits on the first eighth note of the bar and then snare hits on the third beat. Once this is done, return to the main Arrange page and set your locator positions on either side of the one-bar block. Press Cycle on the main Transport bar and you should hear a repeating 5/8 rhythm.

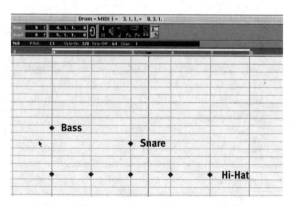

Cubase Drum Editor showing a 5/8 recorded rhythm

Tutorial 26: Recording A 3/4 Pattern

1   Keep your sequencer's quantise setting as eighth notes and change the time-signature setting to '3/4'.

2   Select a track on which to record your hi-hats in the usual way. This time, record a one-bar pattern that plays on the first quarter note only. Your count-in will be 'one-two-three'.

3   Double-click on the recorded hi-hat part and move into your editing window. Using either the Pencil or the Drumstick tool, place the hi-hat on the first quarter note and punch in your bass-drum hits (on the first quarter note) and your snare hits (on the second and third quarter notes). The end result should look like the screenshot on the next page.

4   Return to the main Arrange page, set your locator positions to either side of the one-bar block and press Cycle. You should hear a repeating 3/4 pattern.

Odd Times

The above tutorials highlight the basic rhythmic templates for recording in odd time signatures. Once you've done the basic programming, you can start to add other notes, as previous tutorials have shown.

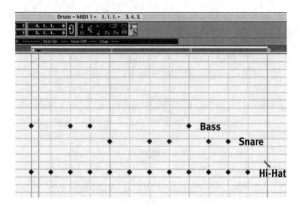

Cubase Drum Editor showing a 3/4 recorded rhythm

You should treat rhythms in odd time signatures in exactly the same way as you would more common rhythms – the same subdivision theory applies. Also, the same quantise settings can be applied to rhythmic templates of odd times.

Time And Tempo Changes Within An Arrangement

In many arrangements, there may well be a need to apply a change in time signature or tempo. In Cubase, you have a choice of two windows in which this can be achieved: the Mastertrack List Editor and the Mastertrack Graphic Editor.

The Mastertrack List Editor can be opened by going to the Edit menu and selecting List Editor or by pressing Ctrl (Apple Command) + M on the keyboard.

Here you can change both the time signature and the tempo of a track by clicking on the Event List with the cursor. You can also adjust where in the arrangement these changes occur by altering the Meter Position List to the left of the dialog box by clicking on it.

A great way of naturally slowing down or speeding up an arrangement is by making use of the Record Tempo facility, which enables you to alter the tempo of an arrangement and record it. The changes can then be edited in the Mastertrack List Editor later on. Here's how you do this:

1   On the Transport bar, click on the Mastertrack icon.

2   Select Record Tempo/Mutes from the Options menu.

3   Return to the start of the arrangement and press Record.

You can now adjust the tempo by using the + and − keys on the keypad and the changes will be recorded by Cubase.

The Cubase Mastertrack List Editor

Meanwhile, the Mastertrack Graphic Editor shows you exactly what changes are occurring to the tempo and time signature of an arrangement as it progresses.

To change the time signature of an arrangement at a particular point, click on the Time Signature strip using the Pencil tool and a time-signature hit point will be

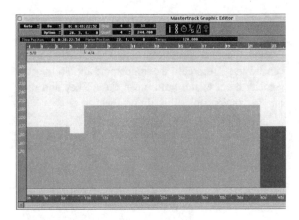

The Cubase Mastertrack Graphic Editor

inserted. You can change the time signature value at a particular point by illuminating the 'I' icon on the Info bar and clicking on your chosen time signature point with the mouse – the time-signature values will nudge up or down accordingly. Remember that any changes in time signature can be erased using the Eraser tool.

You can also use the Pencil tool to increase or decrease the tempo of an arrangement. For instance, if you wish to change the tempo of a particular section of your arrangement, hold down the Alt key and, using the Pencil tool, select the event that you want to change.

basic Rhythm Programming

The accuracy of your editing is determined by the snap value selected in the Snap dialog box at the top of the Graphic Mastertrack Editor. Also, the Crosshairs tool can be used to create a tempo ramp by altering the velocity data. Again, hold down the Alt key and drag the Crosshairs tool either up or down.

Also available from **smt**

BASIC CUBASE SX

Michael Prochak | £6.99 | $7.95 | 1-84492-008-9

BASIC MACWORLD MUSIC HANDBOOK

Michael Prochak | £5 | $7.95 | 1-86074-427-3

BASIC DIGITAL RECORDING

Paul White | £5.99 | $8.95 | 1-86074-269-6

BASIC VST INSTRUMENTS

Paul White | £5 | $7.95 | 1-86074-360-9

BASIC VST EFFECTS

Paul White | £5 | $7.95 | 1-86074-359-5

BASIC SAMPLING

Paul White | £5.99 | $8.95 | 1-86074-477-X

CUBASE SX - THE OFFICIAL GUIDE

Michael Prochak | £11.95 | $17.95 | 1-86074-470-2

MACWORLD MUSIC HANDBOOK

Michael Prochak | £20 | $28 | 1-86074-319-6

FOR MORE INFORMATION on titles from Sanctuary Publishing, visit www.sanctuarypublishing.com or contact us at: Sanctuary House, 45-53 Sinclair Road, London W14 0NS. Tel: +44 (0)20 7602 6351

To order a title direct, call our sales department or write to the above address. You can also order from our website at www.sanctuarypublishing.com